Augustus Henry Keane

Handbook of the History of the English Language

For the Use of Teacher and Student. Fourth Edition

Augustus Henry Keane

Handbook of the History of the English Language
For the Use of Teacher and Student. Fourth Edition

ISBN/EAN: 9783337086435

Printed in Europe, USA, Canada, Australia, Japan

Cover: Foto ©Thomas Meinert / pixelio.de

More available books at **www.hansebooks.com**

THE
ENGLISH LANGUAGE

LONDON: PRINTED BY
SPOTTISWOODE AND CO., NEW-STREET SQUARE
AND PARLIAMENT STREET

HANDBOOK OF THE HISTORY

OF THE

ENGLISH LANGUAGE

FOR THE USE OF TEACHER AND STUDENT

BY

A. H. KEANE, B.A.

AUTHOR OF 'FRENCH ACCENT'
'THE TRUE THEORY OF GERMAN DECLENSION AND CONJUGATION'
ETC.

'The ground of our own language appertaineth to this old Saxon'—CAMDEN

FOURTH EDITION, ENLARGED AND REVISED

LONDON
LONGMANS, GREEN, AND CO.
1878

PREFACE

TO

THE PRESENT EDITION.

Since the first appearance of this work the field of English philology has been sedulously cultivated by many able writers both at home and abroad. It may be sufficient here to mention Koch's 'Historische Grammatik,' 1869; Mätzner's 'Englische Grammatik,' 1865; Marsh's 'English Language,' 1862; Helfenstein's 'Comparative Grammar of the Teutonic Languages,' 1870; Dr. Abbott's 'Shakspearian Grammar,' 1870; Dr. Morris's 'Historical Outlines,' 1873; A. J. Ellis's great work on 'Early English Pronunciation,' 1868–75; and the important Transactions of the Chaucer and Early English Text Societies. These and several other recent works have been consulted in the preparation of the present edition, which thus embodies much fresh matter in further illustration of the successive steps by which the English tongue has arrived at its present state.

Some may possibly affect surprise that no change has been made in the nomenclature, and that the terms *Saxon* and *Anglo-Saxon* are still retained. But after mature deliberation I am more than ever convinced that the outcry raised by Mr. Freeman, Mr. Sweet, Dr. Morris, and a few others against these names, is unreasonable, and that their contentions cannot be upheld. It might be supposed that if there ever were Teuton tribes calling themselves Saxons, and not merely called so by others, it would be childish to quibble about the term Saxon as applied to the Teuton dialects spoken by them. But Mr. Freeman will hear of nothing but *English*, on the ground that 'as far as we can go back, that language has always had the same name, and that name has been English.' And in his 'Historical Outlines,' Dr. Morris* goes still further. 'These Teutonic invaders,' he says, 'were known to the Romans and Celts by the name of Saxons ; and this term was afterwards applied by them to the Teutonic settlers of the fifth century ; *who, however, never appear to have called themselves Saxons*, but always *Anglisc* or English' (p. 28).

Than this it may be doubted whether any more reckless statement ever was made by an otherwise really accomplished scholar. Apart from the broad fact that it was the Saxons themselves, and not the Welsh or other foreigners, that mapped out the parts of the island settled by them into the various kingdoms or political divisions of the East Saxons, the West Saxons, the South Saxons, &c. (names still living in our Sussex, Essex, Middlesex), endless passages might be quoted from the very earliest writers, from charters, laws, and authentic documents of all sorts, showing that the word

---

* In later works, however, Dr. Morris gives up the point, and quietly returns to the use of the really indispensable terms Saxon and Anglo-Saxon. Thus, at p. 32 of the Preface to his Chaucer (1874), we have: 'In Anglo-Saxon *fader, brother, doughter* took no inflexion in the singular.' And again: 'This construction occurs in A.S. writers,' p. 36; 'verbs of Saxon origin,' p. 37, and elsewhere *passim*.

Saxon was freely used in Saxon times and by Saxon writers, as applicable both to the people and to their language. Thus in the '*Wid-sið*,' one of the oldest, if not the very oldest, piece of Saxon poetry extant, the *Scop* or 'Widewanderer' tells us that amongst the many tribes and peoples visited by him were the *Saxons*: 'And mid Ænum and mid Seaxum ic wæs:' p. 322 of Thorpe's 'Codex Exoniensis.' In the same poem, and probably for the first time in an English text, *Angle* occurs under the forms *Ongle* and *Engle* four times: Offa weold Ongle; mid englum ic wæs, &c.

But as soon as both tribes could be spoken of as one people we find *both terms from the very first used indifferently* by English writers when speaking comprehensively of all the Teutonic tribes settled in Britain. Thus, our very earliest historian, Bede: 'Gens Anglorum SIVE Saxonum Britanniam tribus longis navibus advehitur.' Chronicon, A. 449, p. 163, in Stevenson's edition, 1841. And in his 'Hist. Eccl.' I. 22: 'Genti Saxonum SIVE Anglorum,'* here placing the Saxons before the Angles, though himself an Anglian. In his Life of Hwætberht he also preserves a letter addressed by that Abbot to the Pope, in which the whole of England is actually spoken of as *Saxony* : ' Hwætberchtus...Abbas Cœnobii beatissimi Apostolorum principis Petri in SAXONIA.' Bedæ Opera Hist. II., p. 159. So also Gregory I. in a Brief ad An. 596 : ' SAXONIA transmarina,'†

* So also Alfred translates the expression 'historiam gentis Anglorum,' at the opening of Bede's History: 'Angel þcôde and Seaxum,' supplying the word *Saxon*, as if he had not yet brought himself to look upon *Angel* as alone sufficient to include the whole people.

† With these passages compare also: ' Ego Leutherius gr. D. episcopus pontificatus SAXONIÆ gubernacula regens' (A. 675, in Cod. Diplomaticus, I. p. 14); Ego Ini monarchus SAXONIÆ, A. 699, *ib*.,

though both he and Bede more generally use the words *Anglia* and *Anglus*—the Roman bishop because he seems to have first become acquainted with Anglians, and the historian because he was an Anglian. As, moreover, Anglian letters prevailed in the eighth century, the word became current even amongst Saxon or Southern writers, and is consequently usually employed by Alfred in speaking of the whole nation. So in a note to the passage 'and we secgað to soðan þæt se tima wæs gesælig and wynsum on Angel-cynne. þa þa Eadgar cyning þone cristen dóm gefyrðrode,' occurring in the Gloucester fragment of St. Swiðhun, its editor, Mr. J. Earle, justly remarks : 'The Saxons called their nation *Angel-cyn*, and their speech *Englisc*. This shows what an influence the Anglian superiority of the seventh and eighth centuries had exercised over the island :' p. 17.

But that Saxony was equally used as applicable to the whole people is sufficiently proved by the above quoted passages. The following will further show that they spoke of their language also as *Saxon* as well as Angle : ' Etiam similiter et a pastu et refectione illorum hominum quos SAXONICE nominamus walhfæred and heora festing and ealra Angelcynnes monna, &c.,' in a deed referred by Kemble to

p. 53 ; Ego Ini rex Saxonum, A. 701 ; SAXONICÆ gentis, p. 62 ; *Angul-Saxonia* (V. p. 169); Angul-Scaxná (II. p. 304); *Ongol-Saxná-cyning*, *i.e.*, Æðelstan (V. 218). And in a rare old Lambeth MS. of the N. T. given by Maelbride Mac Durnan, bishop of Armagh, 885-927, to this same king Æthelstan, and by him to the Church of Canterbury for ever, there occurs the expression ' Athelstanus Anglo-Saexna Rex, 925,' where the Saxon gen. pl. *na* for the Latin *num* (Anglo-Saexna for Anglo-Saxonum) should be noted, as implying a very general use of this compound term at the time. Similar instances may be seen in a paper by Fr. A. March, entitled, 'Is there an Anglo-Saxon Language?' in the *Transactions of the American Philological Association for* 1872.

the year 855 (Cod. Dipl. Introd. 42). And in the same place occurs a still more pointed expression from a document of Æðelberht's bearing date 863 : ' Hæc sunt pascua porcorum, que NOSTRA LINGUA SAXHONICA denbera nominamus.' Have these passages escaped the industry of Mr. Freeman, or does he suppose that they can be explained away by his usual device of attributing the use of the term Saxon in this sense to the Welsh and other foreigners? A similar expression occurs in the Chronicler Æthelweard, speaking of the time of the first invaders : ' Porro Anglia vetus sita est inter Saxones et Giotos habens oppidum capitale quod SERMONE SAXONICO Slesuuic nuncupatur, secundum vero Danos Haithaby.' Here the distinction is very obvious which the writer draws on the one hand between the language of the Angles and the Saxons, which he calls 'the Saxon language,' and that of the Danes on the other. So also our first grammarian Ælfric : ' Hæresis, Kyre vel gedwelo-æfterfelgund secund. SAXON. hæreticus,' at p. 55 of the Glossary attached to his Gram. Latino-Saxonica, Oxford, 1659. Bede also, and the Saxon Chronicle, which always has been called the Saxon, not the English, Chronicle, distinguish, whenever necessary, between the Saxon and the Anglian dialects, as in Hist. Eccl., II., 5 : ' Caelin rex Occidentalium Saxonum qui LINGUA EORUM Ceawlin vocabatur.' Nor should it be forgotten that this West-Saxon language, here spoken of, took precedence of the Northumbrian, or Anglian proper, in the ninth century, and that in it, rather than in Anglisc, are in fact composed nearly all the extant remains of our earliest literature, though the terms Anglian* and Anglisc,

* With regard to these terms themselves—Angle, Anglisc, Englisc, Angel-cyn, &c.—a good deal of misconception seems to exist, which it may be well to clear up. Thus the following passage from the Saxon already consecrated, as it were, by the writings of Bede and of his translator Alfred, continued to prevail. But the Chronicle shows that even the compound *Angel-cyn* does not always and necessarily embrace all the tribes, Angles, Saxons, Jutes, Frisians, as is generally assumed : ' Her ongon Ceowulf ricsian on West-Seaxum and symble he feaht and won oððe wið Angel-cyn oððe wið Wealas,' A. 597. Others again propose to substitute the form *Englisc* for the Saxon period of the language, on the supposition that it differs in sound as well as in spelling from the modern *English*. But here a distinction is necessary. The combination *sc* was certainly pronounced *sk* in the North, but very probably *sh* in the South, so that the term *Englisc* in Alfred's mouth sounded very much as it does to this day. That this sound *sh* is recent, I hold to be utterly untenable, notwithstanding the great weight of certain names to the contrary.* It may also be noted that the first letter *e* is simply the Southern *anlaut* or modification of the Northern *a* : *Englisc* for *Anglisc*, like *Ælfred*, *Ælfric*, for *Alfred*, *Alfric* ; whence also England for *Angland* = *Anglaland* = the land of the Angles. Most foreign nations have accepted this change at our hands, calling us *Englisch* (German), *Inglese* (Ital.), *Ingles* (Span.), &c. But our more immediate neighbours, the French, still adhere to the older or Northern forms, *Anglais*, *Angleterre*, probably translating directly from the Latin *Anglus*, *Anglia*. This form also has found its way into the East, where we are known to the natives of India as اَنگریزی = Angrēzī for *Anglesi*, *l* interchanging with *r*, as in the French *orme*, *apôtre*, *épître*, and in this very word *Ingrese*, which is often heard amongst the lower classes for *Inglese* in many parts of Italy. *English* therefore is simply the Southern form of the Northern *Anglish* or *Anglisc*, and is the proper name of the *Anglian* or *Northern* dialect, commonly, though not exclusively, applied also to the West-Saxon and other Southern dialects, finally to any form of Saxon or Early English, mainly through the influence of our first writers, Cadmon, Bede, probably also Cynewulf, who happened to be Angles, and not Saxons. But it must be now evident that it would be more correct, besides being vastly more convenient, to restrict *Anglisc* to the Northern dialect, and to designate the old Southern language that has come down to us in literature by its proper name of Saxon, as had been the uniform practice of all writers on the subject till Mr. Freeman started his hobby.

authorities here quoted show that the corresponding term Saxon is fully justified by historic use, and being in all other respects far more convenient and correct, it has been accordingly retained in the present edition of this work, herein agreeing with the uniform practice of all writers on the Anglo-Saxon language from Hickes down to the present day, including such names as Wanley, Ingram, Elstob, the Conybeares, Turner, Bosworth, Kemble, Stephens, Thorpe, Earle, and all American and foreign writers without exception.

To the present edition have been added two appendices. The first contains twelve versions, synoptically arranged, of the Lord's Prayer, at different periods, from the earliest times till the sixteenth century. It will help to show in a concrete form the various phases through which the language has passed, and thus serve as a general illustration of its history, as briefly set forth in these pages. The second consists of a digest or summary of all existing Saxon and English remains down to the beginning of the fourteenth century It includes an account of the extant MSS., their probable date, dialect in which written, when, where, and by whom first published, all arranged as far as possible in chronological order. The teacher may find it useful for purposes of reference, and the student as a lesson in accuracy.

PREFACE

TO

THE FIRST EDITION.

THE History of the English Language, as distinct from that of its Literature, constitutes a separate division of the English department at the Civil Service and other Government examinations. An effort has been made in the following pages to throw into as small a space as possible all such matter as is needed to meet the requirements of that single head. Indeed the present work was actually suggested by, and has been wholly planned on, the very first question on the English language put to the candidates at the July examinations, 1858. However abstruse, however varied, or seemingly superfluous, the matter herein contained, it is but an answer, and that far from complete, to this remarkable question :—' Give a distinct account of the constitution of the English language, in respect both of the vocabulary and of the grammar, at each of the following dates: in the tenth century, when it was still what is usually called Saxon or Anglo-Saxon by modern philologists' (see the whole of Sec. II.); 'in the twelfth' (Sec. III.); 'in the fourteenth' (Sec. V.); 'in the sixteenth and in the eighteenth'

(Sec. VI.); noting carefully the difference between each stage of its progress, and the immediate preceding one, and assigning the cause or causes of the change.'

But, while the whole book is thus occupied in dealing with this formidable query, it may have incidentally disposed of others less exacting in their nature, *ex. gr.* second :— 'Describe clearly and exactly the position and connexion of the English language (regarded in its earliest known form, which is still its basis or mould), in what is called the Indo-European family of languages' (Sec. I.); the fourth :—' Compare the English language in its present state with any other, ancient or modern, with which you may be familiar, in general serviceableness and power as an instrument of expression' (Sec. VI., § 97, 98); the fifth :—' Illustrate by a few decisive examples the manner in which the English language adopts words from the French (Sec. V., § 72 ; VI., § 95), from the Latin (Sec. VI., § 97), and from the Greek (Sec. VI., § 99) languages respectively; and the nature of the changes, whether in the spelling, the pronunciation, or both, by which it assimilates them, and makes them its own.'

But though the work has been planned and the subject matter selected with a view to meet the requirements of these examinations, its special object may not, perhaps, render it the less generally useful, having been so compiled as to form a practical introduction both to the history of English literature and to an exact knowledge of the science of English grammar. It may thus be found a valuable text-book to the more advanced pupils of our schools and colleges, without being altogether void of interest to the general reader. A knowledge of the steps by which the language has reached its present state seems needed to the right understanding of the true principles of English grammar. Changes like *its* for *his, they* for *hi, loving* for *lovand,* are intelligible only in the light of the past; and it may be truly said that if nearly all our grammars are avowedly meaningless, often positively injurious, it is because they treat the language either in conformity with a classic model or with a total disregard of its past history and Saxon origin.

CONTENTS.

                                                                    PAGE
PREFACE to Present Edition. Use of the terms Saxon and Anglo-Saxon defended against the objections of Mr. Freeman, Dr. Morris, and others   v
PREFACE to First Edition. Object and plan of the work .   xiii

SECTION I.
INTRODUCTORY. §§ 1–11.

Paragraphs 1–2. Philology—Families of Languages . . .   1
   3. Finno-Tataric Family   3
   4. Indo-European or Aryan Family   5
   5. Keltic Branch   6
   6. Teutonic Branch   6
   7. The Low German Tribes—Frisians   7
   8. The Jutes   9
   9. The Angles and Saxons 10
 10. The Term Anglo-Saxon 11
 11. The Angles 12
    Questions 13

SECTION II.
ANGLO-SAXON PERIOD. §§ 12–31.

12. Periods of the English Language 15
13. Anglo-Saxon Alphabet 16
14. Its Origin 18
15. Saxon Orthography and Accent 18
16. Saxon a Synthetic Language 19
17. Grammar—Definite Adjective 20
18. Gender and Declension 21
19. Origin of the Modern Possessive and Plural . . . 22

xviii *Contents.*

	PAGE
20. Indefinite Adjective	23
21. Degrees of Comparison	24
22. Pronouns	24
23. Verb	25
24. Grammatical Exercise	27
25. Vocabulary—Keltic Element	29
26. Latin Element. The word *Church*	31
27. Norse Element	32
28. Traces of Dialects—'Dano-Saxon'	34
29. Poetic System—Laws of Alliteration	35
30. Rhyme—Its probable origin	36
31. Specimens of Saxon Prose and Verse. Cadmon—Alfred—Ælfric—Saxon Chronicle—West Saxon and Northumbrian Gospels	37
Questions	43

SECTION III.
BROKEN SAXON PERIOD. §§ 32-45

32. Dates	45
33. Two Languages—the Written and Spoken	46
34. Various Theories to account for the Corruption of Anglo-Saxon	47
35. Analysis and Synthesis	49
36. Downward Tendency of Anglo-Saxon	51
37. Norman Influence	51
38. Influence of the Monks	52
39. The Grammar of this Period—Verb	54
40. Noun—Possessive and Plural	55
41. Adjective—Gender—Pronoun	56
42. Vocabulary of this Period	57
43. Specimens. Saxon Chronicle	58
44. Layamon	61
45. A Rhyming Poem—the Moral Ode	62
Questions	65

SECTION IV.
EARLY ENGLISH PERIOD. §§ 46-59.

46. Nature and Extent of this Period	66
47. Fusion of Saxon and Norman Elements	67
48. Change of Alphabet—Orthography	68

		PAGE
49.	Various Languages employed in Literature	69
50.	Difference between Broken Saxon and Early English	70
51.	Grammar—Final *e* Syllabic	72
52.	Infinitive—Gerund—Present Participle	73
53.	Comparative Table of Early English Forms	75
54.	Vocabulary—Norman Element	75
55.	Romance and Latin Element	78
56.	The Ormulum—its date	81
57.	Its Orthography—pronunciation	82
58.	Specimens. The Ormulum—Alliterative Ode—Ballad	84
59.	Robert Mannyng—the Proclamation of Henry III.	87
	Supplement to the Grammar of the Transition Period—Changes from 1100 to 1150—Changes from 1150 to 1250—Changes from 1250 to 1300	89
	Questions	91

SECTION V.

MIDDLE ENGLISH PERIOD. §§ 60-78.

60.	Extent of this Period	93
61.	Difference between Early and Middle English	94
62.	Final *e*—when pronounced	95
63.	Final *e* French—Accent	96
64.	Grammatical and Orthographic value of final *e*	97
65.	Middle English Noun—Possessive—Plural	98
66.	Pronoun—Infinitive—Past Participle	99
67.	Present Indicative	100
68.	Past Tense—Imperative	101
69.	Help Verbs—*to have, to be, shall, will,* &c.	102
70.	Gerund and Modern Infinitive	103
71.	Proclamation of Edward III.—Recognition of English as the National Speech	104
72.	Late Introduction of Norman Words	106
73.	How accounted for	107
74.	Specimens. Two Rival Schools of Literature, the Norman and Saxon	109
75.	Piers Ploughman's Vision and Creed	110
76.	Chaucer—his Poetic System, Grammar, and Vocabulary	113
77.	Specimens of Prose. Mandeville—Trevisa	116
78.	Barbour—Lowland Dialect	118
	Questions	122

SECTION VI.

MODERN ENGLISH PERIOD. §§ 79-102.

		PAGE
79.	Extent of this Period	124
80.	First Modern Writers—Lydgate—James I.—Scotch and Ballad Poetry	125
81.	Caxton—Introduction of Printing—Sir Thomas More	128
82.	Effects of the Art of Printing	129
83.	Unsettled state of the Orthography	131
84.	Three causes of irregularity: change of alphabet, change of pronunciation, defective alphabet	132
85.	Grammar—number of actual endings in Modern English	135
86.	Historical Table of English Accidence	137
87.	Anomalous Forms—plurals in *en*	142
88.	Three dialects: Northern, Midland, Southern	143
89.	The Modern Pronouns—*it* and *its*	144
90.	The forms *they, their, them, my, thy*, &c.	145
91.	Verbal forms—Present Indicative—Participles	147
92.	Relational Words—their real nature	149
93.	Vocabulary—Saxon and Romance Elements	150
94.	Preponderance of the Saxon Element	152
95.	The four Periods of the Romance Element	154
96.	Causes of the Composite Character of Modern English	156
97.	Analysis of the Romance Element	159
98.	Synonyms	161
99.	Greek Element	162
100.	Miscellaneous Element	163
101.	Style—Generic and Specific Terms—Platitudes	165
102.	Present Position and Future Prospects of the English Language	168
	Questions	170

APPENDIX I.

Twelve Versions of the Lord's Prayer from the Eighth to the Sixteenth Century, synoptically arranged 173

APPENDIX II.

A DIGEST of Early English Remains, from Beowulf to Mannyng 178

THE
ENGLISH LANGUAGE.

SECTION I.

INTRODUCTORY.

PRELIMINARY OBSERVATIONS ON PHILOLOGICAL STUDIES—THEIR IMPORTANCE — CLASSIFICATION OF EUROPEAN LANGUAGES — INDO-EUROPEAN OR ARYAN FAMILY — TEUTONIC BRANCH — ANGLO-SAXON.

PHILOLOGY—FAMILIES OF LANGUAGES.

1. ALTHOUGH this section is called introductory, the matter it treats of should not, therefore, be underrated or passed over lightly. It is, indeed, only preliminary to the main subject; yet as necessary to its right understanding as is the doorway to him who would enter a dwelling. We can have no clear notion of the structure of the English language considered in itself, or of its position in relation to others, without some acquaintance with the general principles of philology. This study has somewhere been called *speech-knowledge*. The term, though it has not been generally received, yet conveys, perhaps, a more accurate notion of the true nature and object of this department of learning in its present improved state, than is expressed by the more classic denomination. For it professes to treat of and expound the principles on which language is formed, and thus to give us a clearer insight into the structure, and a more exact *knowledge*, of *speech* in general. Comparative

philology goes a step further. It applies to language, in the aggregate, the laws which regulate it in its absolute condition ; and in the hands of the Christian philosopher, can have but one object in view—to demonstrate the ultimate identity of all human speech, even as we believe in the one origin of all mankind.

2. This most interesting of studies is of very recent date, and is still in its infancy. It has only grown into the dignity of a science during the present century, a very long time having been necessarily spent in collecting the materials and facts it required as a groundwork on which to build up and verify its theories. Yet, the triumphs it has achieved within the last few years are truly wonderful. Nearly all the known languages of the world have been already classified, or reduced to a certain number of great stocks, as a first step towards tracing all back to one common source. The European languages are all comprised in two of these, which further include a vast number of Asiatic tongues. In other words, all the languages of Europe, together with more than half of those of Asia, are derived from two sources, originally and radically distinct. Some two languages at some very remote period were spoken, to which all these are directly or indirectly reducible, each aggregate constituting what in Philology is called a *family* of languages. The chief subdivisions of a family are called *branches*. A family bears the same relation to all its branches that a branch does to all its *dialects*. Logically a family is a *genus*, comprising so many branches or *species*, which again embrace an indefinite number of *individual* dialects. Our two families or genera are called :—

(*a*) Finno-Tataric.
(*b*) Indo-European, or Aryan.

Any language which is directly traceable to any other in (*a*) or in (*b*), is said to be a *dialect* of that. In this sense French may be said to be a dialect of Latin. Any language which cannot be directly traced to any other in (*a*) or (*b*), but which can be shown to belong to (*a*) or (*b*), is said to be a *branch*. Latin is a branch of (*b*). Were we to lose all knowledge of the fact that ever such a language existed as Latin, the Romance tongues, French, Spanish, Italian, would cease to be *dialects*—would be grouped together, and would constitute a *branch* of (*b*). The great problem in comparative philology is to reduce (*a*), (*b*), (*c*), (*d*) . . . . to (x) = genus supremum = unity.*

THE FINNO-TATARIC FAMILY.

3. (*a*) The Finno-Tataric family is believed to be the most ancient in Europe, and to have at one time occupied a wider geographical area than any other in the world. In pre-historic times it is supposed to have spread over the greater portion of Europe; but, as far back as history goes, we find it already driven into the extremities north and south by the Indo-European race. At present, in its widest

---

* The possibility of reducing all forms of speech to one source has, of course, been questioned, nor can anyone pretend to assert positively that the problem ever will be solved. Yet it is well to keep it constantly in view, and to note the progress that is being made from time to time towards its solution. A decided step in advance is marked by Raabe's 'Gemeinschaftliche Grammatik der Arischen und der Semitischen Sprachen,' Leipzig, 1874. In this work the author feels himself justified in substituting 'gemeinschaftlich' or common for 'vergleichend,' or comparative, and boldly asserts that 'although some investigators maintain the impossibility of discovering an organic union between the Indo-Germanic and the Semitic families, yet even apart from my work a connecting link (Zusammenhang) will be found to exist between the two.'—Preface. He himself identifies many roots as common to both, whose affinity had not hitherto been recognised, as for instance the Sanscrit *çûshâ* = snorting, with the Hebrew סוּס *sûs*, a horse. He goes even further, and expresses his belief that the Coptic or Old Egyptian itself is nothing but a *disguised Sanscrit*, 'ein verhülltes Sanskrit.' His promised 'Hebrew-Aryan' Dictionary will be looked forward to with great interest.

I.—*Introductory*.

extent, it consists of five well-defined *branches*, which give the following scheme :—

a = Genus = Stock Language of the Finno-Tataric Family.

1. Tchudic.   2. Jakuto-Turkish.   3. Samojede.   4. Tataro-Mongolian.   5. Tungus.

I. *Tchudic* branch : (1) Finnic proper, Esthonian, Lapp of Lapland; (2) Permian; (3) Volga Finn; (4) Magyar of Hungary.

II. *Jakuto-Turkish* branch: (1) Old Turkish on the Mongolian frontier, Osmanli; (2) Turkoman (from Balk to the Caspian); (3) Yakutish (in Siberia).

III. *Samojede* branch: Ostjak; Yennissei Samojede (nomad tribes on the shores of the Arctic, stretching from Archangel eastwards).

IV. *Tataro-Mongolian* branch: (1) East Mongolian (about the desert of Gobi); (2) Kalmuk (in the great steppes of West Asia, and on the Lower Volga).

V. *Tungus* branch : (1) Siberian Tungus; (2) Mandchoo (spoken by the ruling race in China).

Isolated languages which cannot be shown to belong to any known *family*, are called *sporadic*. There are, or have been until very recently, two such in Europe: the *Basque* and the *Albanian*. The Basque or Euscaric, which is supposed to represent the old Iberian of Spain, is spoken by the Escaldunacs of the Pyrenees. It is now believed to be connected with the Finno-Tataric family, and is used as an argument to prove that Europe was first peopled by this race. The Albanian is spoken in Turkish Albania by the Arnauts, or, as they call themselves, the Skipetari, or Highlanders. They are now generally looked upon as the descendants of the ancient Illyrians, who skirted Greece on the north, and reached from the Adriatic into Asia Minor, including the Dacians, Phrygians, Carians, and Hellenized Macedonians and Epirots. The Skipetar was at one time referred to the Finno-Tataric: it is at present more commonly comprised in the next or Indo-European family.

THE INDO-EUROPEAN, OR ARYAN FAMILY.

4. (*b*) The Indo-European, or Aryan, Family, is the greatest and the most influential, not only in Europe, but in the world. It reaches from the furthest limits of Cisgangetic India, through Persia and Western Asia, to the extreme west of Europe, and has, within a recent date, spread throughout North and South America and Australasia. Its branches are the following six:—

b = Genus = Stock Language of Indo-European Family.

1. Indian. 2. Medo-Persian. 3. Pelasgic. 4. Sclavonian. 5. Keltic. 6. Teutonic.

I. *Indian* branch: (1) *Sanscrit*, the religious language of the Hindoos; (2) *Pali*, the religious language of the Buddhists; (3) *Pracrit*, the vulgar or spoken forms of Sanscrit, now extinct. From these are derived the Hindustani, Bengali, etc., in all about fifty Indian dialects, together with the Gipsy of Europe.

II. *Medo-Persian* branch: (1) *Old Persian*, of the arrow-headed Persepolitan monuments; (2) *Zend*, of Zoroaster's Zend Avesta; (3) *Parsi*, still spoken by the Parsees of Bombay, Modern Persian, Affghan, perhaps Armenian.

III. *Pelasgic* branch: (1) *Greek* and *Romaic*; (2) *Latin* and *Romance* (Italian, French, Spanish, Moldavo-Wallachian). The Daco-Roman inhabitants of the Danubian Principalities are descended from the Roman colony planted in Dacia by Trajan.

IV. *Sclavonian* branch: (1) *Lithuanian*, the best preserved of all living Indo-European tongues; (2) *Russian*; (3) *Polish*; (4) *Bohemian*; (5) *Illyrian*; (6) *Bulgarian*.

V. *Keltic* branch: (1) *Irish*; (2) *Welsh*.

VI. *Teutonic* branch: (1) *Mœso-Gothic*, which possesses the oldest literary remains (A. 380); (2) *Old Frisic*; (3) *Old High German*; (4) *Norse*.

THE KELTIC BRANCH.

5. The first four need not detain us further, as they are not immediately connected with the subject. The Keltic, by those who reject the Finnish theory, is generally allowed to have been the primitive language of Western Europe and of the British Isles. It is subdivided into the two following groups:—

Gaedhelic.	Kymric.
Irish. Manks. Erse.	Welsh. Cornish. Low Breton.

Cornish is now extinct, and the Manks, of the Isle of Man, is fast disappearing. Welsh still holds its ground as the representative of the language universally spoken in Southern Britain, down to the middle of the fifth century. The Gaedhelic, however, seems to have preceded it even in Wales, where Dr. Lhuyd, the great Welsh antiquarian, has shown that the names of the mountains, plains, and rivers, are Irish rather than Kymric. But if it be true, as is now suspected, that the Keltic of Gaul and of the British Isles was still one language at the Christian era, Dr. Lhuyd's statement will only prove that the Keltic of Britain has since then considerably fallen off, and that the Keltic of Ireland has preserved itself in comparative purity.

THE TEUTONIC BRANCH.

6. But by far the most important branch of the Indo-European family, in connection with the present subject, i the Teutonic.

It comprises the three following subdivisions:—

(*a*) High German.
(*b*) Low German.
(*c*) Scandinavian.

(*a*) The *High German* includes all the dialects that prevail on the hilly lands of Southern Germany; such are the

Swiss, Suabian, Bavarian, and German Proper. The stages of this latter are:—

 a. Old High German, spoken in the ninth, tenth, and eleventh centuries in Suabia, Bavaria, and Franconia.

 β. Middle High German, from the twelfth to the sixteenth century.

 γ. New High German, the general literary language of Germany at the present day.

(*b*) The *Low German* embraces all the languages spoken on the plains and coast of Northern Germany, between the Rhine and the Oder. These are principally the Frisian, Old or Continental Saxon, Low Dutch of Holland, Flemish, and the dialects of Hanover, Oldenburgh, Schleswig, and Holstein.

(*c*) To the *Scandinavian branch* belong the *Old Norse*, Icelandic, Feroic, Dalekarlian, Swedish, Danish, and Norwegian. Of these the Icelandic still closely resembles the Norse, having experienced little change since the twelfth century. It is by far the best preserved of all living Teutonic tongues.

THE LOW GERMAN TRIBES—THE FRISIANS.

7. Though there is much difference of opinion amongst writers as to the exact locality of the German tribes that invaded Britain in the fifth century, yet all agree in bringing them from that part of Northern Germany which lies between Western Flanders and Schleswig. The languages which they spoke and introduced into the country must, therefore, have belonged to the *Low German* branch; consequently to it must be referred the Anglo-Saxon and Modern English. Of the Low German dialects, that which most resembles the English to this day is the Frisian. This tongue, at one time generally prevailing from Holland to Jutland, is now broken up into the following varieties:—

 a. Frisian proper, in the province of Frisia; β. Westphalian or Hanoverian Frisian, spoken only in the fenny district of Saterland; γ. Frisian of Heligoland; δ. North Frisian, current in Schleswig. The only one possessing any remains is the first, whose literature dates from the thirteenth century. These Frisians, whose pronunciation resembles that of the west Somersetmen, still look upon the English as their kinsmen, and the resemblance of the two speeches is certainly very remarkable. As a specimen, Mr. Halbertsma gives, in Bosworth's 'Anglo-Saxon Dictionary,' the following Frisian version of one of the Countess of Blessington's songs:—

Hhwat bist dou, libben?	What art thou, life?
Jen wirch stribjen	A weary strife
Fen pine, noed in soárch;	Of pain, care, and sorrow;
Lange oeren fen smerte	Long hours of grief
In nocten ho koart!	And joys, how brief!
Det fordwine de moarns.	That vanish the morrow.
Déad, hwat bist dou,	Death, what art thou,
Ta hwaem allen buwgje,	To whom all bow,
Fen de scepterde kening ta de slawe?	From sceptered king to, slave?

Nor can there be any doubt that the Frisians were among the first invaders of the country. In the 'Life of St. Swibert,' we read: 'Ecgburtus sitiens salutem *Frisonum* et Saxonum, eo quod Angli ab iis propagati sunt.'

The same inference must be drawn from the prevalence of the topographical ending *wick, wich,* in every part of the country: Hawick, Harwich, Warwick, Dulwich, Sandwich, Woolwich, &c.; and which, as Lappenberg remarks, is met with nowhere in Germany except 'in Altsachsen und Friesland,' where, as in Wycombe, Wichfield, it forms the first part of the compound term. He instances Wykgrafen, Wykvogten, Wykscheffeln. Geschichte v. England, I. 85. This term *wick,* though undoubtedly belonging to the same Aryan root as the Latin *vicus,* has been too hastily derived from it by writers who overlooked the fact that it is found in parts of the island never occupied by the Romans, as in Lerwick and Wick, in the extreme north of Scotland.

THE JUTES

8. The other invading tribes, we are told, were the Jutes, Saxons, and Angles, who, coming over at intervals, ultimately succeeded in occupying the whole of what is now called England. These settlements are said to have taken place in the following order :—
 i. Jutes, under Hengist and Horsa, settled in Kent and the Isle of Wight in 449 or 450.
 ii. Saxons, under Ælla, in Suth Seaxna-rice, or Sussex, in 477.
 iii. Saxons, under Cerdic, in West Seaxna-rice, or Wessex, in 493.
 iv. Saxons, in East Seaxna-rice, or Essex, in 530.
 v. Angles, during the reign of Cerdic, in Norfolk and Suffolk, 527.
 vi. Angles, under Ida, between the Tweed and Forth, in 547.

Our principal authority for this statement is the 'Historia Ecclesiastica' of the Venerable Bede, written at the beginning of the eighth century. It thus appears that the Jutes occupied Kent, the Isle of Wight, and a portion of the opposite coast; the Saxons peopled all the rest of the country south of the Thames and of the Avon, besides Essex, Middlesex, and Hertford; the Angles took possession of the remainder of the Island, reaching as far north as the Forth and Clyde, and west to Wales. From these latter it received the name of Ængla-land, or England, although this word would be, according to Thierry, a contraction of the more comprehensive designation Engel-Seaxna-land, just as West Seaxna-rice became Wessex. Until very recently, the Jutes were assumed to have come from Jutland in Denmark; but Dr. Latham has shown that this is a mistake, arising, probably, from a fancied resemblance between the two names. The readings in Bede's MSS. vary considerably. In one place they are called Juti, in another Vitæ, and elsewhere Gutæ. That they could not have been Danes seems quite certain; for not the slightest trace of Danish or Norse is found in the Kentish dialect, of which there are extant remains dating from the fourteenth century. It should, however, be remarked that at the time the Jutes are represented as having come over, and even much later on, the difference between the Low German and Norse tongues was very slight. Alfred, in the ninth century, is said on one occasion to have penetrated into the Danish camp, disguised as a harper, and to have entertained the army with his Saxon songs, because, as the chronicle says, 'Lingua Danorum Anglicanæ loquelæ vicina est.' On the whole it appears highly probable that this *Jutarum natio* of Bede were in reality a tribe of western Goths, who crossed over from Gaul in the fifth century, to assist the southern Britons against the incessant attacks of their northern enemies, the Picts and Scots. They are expressly called Goths in Asser's 'Life of Alfred,' and Gaet in Alfred's own works. If so, they were nearly related to the other two invading tribes.

THE ANGLES AND SAXONS.

9. These, we have seen, were the Saxons and the Angles. Bede tells us that the Saxons came from that district of Germany which was in his time known by the name of the Country of the Old Saxons, that is, the tract lying between the Elbe and the Eider. Yet this is the very region that the Saxon Chronicle points out as the home of the Angles: 'Eald-Seax, **Anglorum** antiqua patria.' In reality, at the time of the invasion there was no substantial difference between these two tribes, not more, perhaps, than between a north countryman and a southern, or than afterwards existed between the Saxons of Essex and the Angles of the adjoining county of Suffolk. Bede himself speaks of them as of one race: 'Anglorum sive Saxonum gens.' It is, moreover, quite certain that they looked upon themselves all along as brethren of one family. It is remarkable that it was a *Saxon*, Egbert, king of Wessex, who first gave the name of *England* to the whole country (830 A.D.). And King Ida's laws recognize only two races, the Welsh and the English. This name seems to have been readily adopted by all the successive invading tribes, and even the so-called Jutes of Kent were termed Engle-kin, that is, of English race. We may conclude, then, with Latham, that the invaders bore two names: *Angle*, designating those tribes that came from the more northern parts of Germany bordering on Denmark, and which they appear as a nation to have preferred; and *Saxon*, by which they were best known to the Romans, Franks, and Kelts. To these latter, indeed, whether Welsh, Highlander, or Irish, they were never known by any other than that of *Sassanach*. To account for this, we should remember that for nearly a century before they effected a permanent settlement in the country, Saxon tribes infested the whole eastern coast of England from the Wash to the Isle of Wight, which from this circumstance was designated as the 'Littus Saxonicum' in the 'Notitia utriusque Imperii,' embracing the history of the empire from the year 369 to 408. Consequently, long before the appearance of the Angles, the term Saxon had become too familiar to the old Britons or Welsh to be ever afterwards set aside for another, especially as both meant much the same thing. From the Britons it passed to the Picts and Irish Scots, who were at that time in the habit of making constant inroads into the southern parts of the island.

THE TERM ANGLO-SAXON.

10. With regard to the term *Anglo-Saxon*, Mr. Craik remarks, in his excellent 'Outlines of the English Language,' that, 'whether as applied to the language or to the people by whom it was spoken, it must be understood to mean, properly, Saxon of England as distinguished from Saxon of the Continent; just as Anglo-Norman means Norman of England as distinguished from Norman of the Continent. It is a compound formed on the principle of assuming Saxon as the name of the people and of the language, and England as that of the country. The Anglo-Saxon is merely one dialect of Saxon, as the Continental or Old Saxon is another. It cannot mean, as is sometimes supposed, the language of the Angles and Saxons.' And in the advertisement to the third edition of his work he says that he has everywhere discarded the terms *Saxon* and *Anglo-Saxon*, 'as not only unauthorised by the facts of the case, but absurd and eminently misleading.' Yet this time-honoured compound does seem to us by no means absurd, and sufficiently intelligible withal. It need not mean the Saxon of England, in the same way that Anglo-Norman denotes the Norman of England, or the Anglicised Norman; but, when applied to the people, it very fittingly designates a nation that has been formed by the blending of the two distinct tribes of Angles and Saxons; and when applied to the language, it means not the Saxon of England, as opposed to that of the mainland, but the speech which was common to the two tribes from the beginning, and which was as much *Angle* as it was Saxon. Anglo-Norman implies a corrupt or English-Norman. Anglo-Saxon does not imply a corrupt or English-Saxon, but Angle+Saxon as a nation, Angle=Saxon as a language.

THE ANGLES.

11. The Angles are generally believed to have emigrated from the small territory still known by the name of Anglen, in the duchy of Schleswig. But much importance cannot be attached to this statement. It is not easy to understand how such a narrow tract as Anglen could have supplied the numerous bands of invaders who from time to time poured into England, even though we suppose with Bede that it was left unpeopled for several generations afterwards. In reality such terms as Angle, and Saxon, and Frank, and Goth, were not then so much geographical, denoting fixed or even pure populations, as the names of roving tribes, often formed by a mixture of several nations, and ever shifting to and fro. So the Angles, as Alfred tells us in 'Orosius,' were not restricted to any particular spot, but spread over the whole of the modern kingdom of Denmark, Jutland, Zealand and neighbouring islands: on thám landum eardodon Engle aer hi hider on land comon, *i.e.*, in those lands dwelt the Angles ere they hither-land came. Bede's assertion may now be explained as meaning that those countries remained unoccupied after the departure of the Angles until they were subsequently repeopled by men of Scandinavian race.

QUESTIONS.*

[The numbers refer to those of the paragraphs in each Section.]

1. What is the nature and object of Philology in general? In what does it differ from Comparative Philology?

2. In Philology, what is a *family?* a *branch?* a *dialect?* How many families in Europe?

3. What are the branches of the Finno-Tataric? What is a sporadic language? How many in Europe? Who are the Basques? the Albanians? the Magyars?

4. Name the principal regions occupied by the Indo-European family. How is it distributed? Who are the Wallachians?

5. State the two subdivisions of the Keltic branch, with their respective dialects. Who are supposed to have been the earliest inhabitants of Britain?

---

* These, and following series of questions, are only suggestive, and intended as a guide, especially to teachers. They may occasionally help to draw attention to important matter, which might otherwise pass unnoticed in the perusal of the text.

6. Mention the three off-shoots of the Teutonic branch. Which is the purest of all living Teutonic languages?

7. To which of the Teutonic subdivisions do you refer the Anglo-Saxon? Why? What modern German language resembles most the English?

8. Name the three principal German tribes that invaded Britain in the fifth century. How did they occupy the country? There are reasons for believing that the Jutes had nothing to do with the modern Jutland: who does Dr. Latham think they were?

9. Show that there was no real difference between the Saxons and the Angles. The English are still called Sassanach by all the Kelts: account for this.

10. Mr. Craik's objection to the use of the compound term Anglo-Saxon seems to be unfounded: justify its use.

11. What is to be thought of the statement that the Angles came from Anglen in Schleswig?

SECTION II.

ANGLO-SAXON PERIOD (450-1066).

PERIODS OF THE ENGLISH LANGUAGE—ANGLO-SAXON PERIOD—ALPHABET—ORTHOGRAPHY—GRAMMAR—ITS SYNTHETIC CHARACTER—VOCABULARY—FOREIGN ELEMENTS—DIALECTS—VERSE—SPECIMENS.

PERIODS OF THE ENGLISH LANGUAGE.

12. The Low German speech, introduced by these different tribes in the fifth century, flourished in the country altogether for about six hundred years, or was as nearly as possible coëxtensive with the sway of those that spoke it (450–1066). A period of decay then set in, the germs of which existed from the beginning, and out of this corruption was gradually developed the language as at present spoken and written. Rightly to understand the connection between the two, between the Anglo-Saxon and its modern English off-shoot, account must be taken of the various steps by which the transition was effected. For the English language, as now spoken, was not the growth of a moment, nor did it suddenly attain to its present high state of perfection. By a consideration alone of the intermediate stages, which at once separate and connect the two extremes, we shall be able to understand how the result was obtained. These stages, or epochs, or periods of the history of the language, are not very easy to fix, because it is often difficult to show the last link of one, and the first of another chain. Hence they vary considerably in different writers. It is obvious, however, at first sight, that there can be but three really distinct divisions of the subject, the two fixed extremes—Anglo-Saxon and Modern English—together with the unsettled and ever-changing middle state, the Borderland, between these two. These three different states of the language have been called by various names. The first, that of *Pure*, or *Simple*, or *Saxon*-English; the second, that of *Broken*, or *Ungrammatical*, or *Semi*-English; the third, that of *New*, or *Modern*, or *Mixed*-English. The second alone can occasion any difficulty. It is usually and conveniently subdivided into three others, which, with the first and third, will give us the following periods to be investigated:—

Periods.

I. Anglo-Saxon,	A.D.	450,	lasted	600 years,	till
II. Broken Saxon,		1066,	,,	150	,,
III. Early English,		1200,	,,	150	,,
IV. Middle English,		1350,	,,	100	,,
V. Modern English,		1450,	,,	—	,,

ANGLO-SAXON ALPHABET.

13. We shall never be able to form any notion of the difference between our language and the Anglo-Saxon, and of how the change was effected, unless we be content to go back and see what the original really was. Indeed, the importance of some acquaintance with the Anglo-Saxon can hardly be overrated. It is beyond all doubt the very best means of acquiring a thorough knowledge of the structure of our own speech; for it is to us what Latin is to the Italians, French, and Spaniards—what Old Norse is to the Danes and Swedes. One cause, perhaps, of the neglect into which Anglo-Saxon studies have fallen, is the fact of their having employed a form of writing different from the present. It was assumed practically, that when the old character was laid aside for the modern, the language ceased to be Saxon, and should be studied with reference to a classic model. In reality the Anglo-Saxon alphabet differed but very little from the Latin, of which it was not so much a corruption as a mere variety, or, so to say, a sort of hand employed by the Saxons even in the writing of Latin itself.—Hence, it is now very properly superseded by the modern form, those characters only being retained which were peculiar to it, viz., þ=th hard, as in *thin*, and ð=dh=th soft, as in *then*. As these two letters express sounds of constant occurrence in English, it is much to be regretted that they were not preserved when the transition was effected from the old to the new system. They were, indeed, generally retained in English and Latin MSS. down to the reign of Edward III. But the Norman transcribers of Saxon books always substituted their own orthography for the Anglo-Saxon, and that ultimately prevailed in all cases. The alphabet consisted altogether of twenty-four letters:—

a, as in *fat*.
b.
c, always hard = k, cining = king.   Wuce = week.*
d.
e = ea in b*ea*r.
f = v when between two vowels.   Lufe = luve = love.
g, always hard.   Gifan = give.
h.
i = ee in sheep, probably also = i in wine, and when short = *i* in win;
    before e or u = y : iugoð = youth.
l–m–n–o–p–r–s–t–u–w–x–æ.
y = French u, brýd = bride, or German eu = fýr = fire.
þ = θ = *th* in *thing*.
ð = *dh* = *th*, in *this*.†

---

* In the Hatton MS. of the four Gospels (about 1050) *k* is used instead of *c*: kymð for cymð = cometh. Mark i. 7. (Skeat's 'Synopsis,' Cambridge, 1871.)

† It should, however, be remarked that þ and ð were used very carelessly by Saxon writers. Hickes says that 'hi characteres confunduntur a scriptoribus,' not being carefully distinguished, as in Icelandic, but treated rather as different forms of the same letter, some scribes preferring one and some the other. In the Ormulum we have þ

At the beginning of pronouns and adverbs the modern English substitutes the soft *th*=ð for the hard=þ, as þu= thou, as if from ðu, þær=there, etc., where the change of pronunciation is not observable, because *th* represents both þ and ð.

ITS ORIGIN.

14. Hyde Clarke, in his 'Grammar of the English Tongue,' says that the Anglo-Saxon alphabet 'is likewise found in some Irish books, the Irish having taken this alphabet from our English forefathers.' The very contrary, we venture to say, was the case. To the Irish ' our English forefathers' were indebted for all the literature and learning they possessed, and the Irish, two hundred years before the Anglo-Saxons knew how to read or write, employed this very alphabet, not in *some*, but in all of their books, whether in Latin or in the vernacular. Alban Butler, in his Life of St. Austin, observes that ' the Saxons were a barbarous race, unacquainted even with the art of writing previous to their arrival in England, where they adopted their alphabet from the Irish.' þ, however, is from the Runic.

SAXON ORTHOGRAPHY AND ACCENT.

15. Not one of the least difficulties to the Anglo-Saxon student is the very unsettled state of the orthography. This must be peculiarly perplexing in a language in which a single vowel often changes the case or number of a noun. Rask, who has done much to remedy the evil in his excellent Anglo-Saxon Grammar, describes the orthography as extremely confused, observing that Hickes and Lye, the Saxon editors, have caused it to appear much more so than

only, and in the Hatton MS. of Gregory's Pastorals ð only. This confusion and uncertainty in their use necessarily led later writers to discard them both.

it is in reality, by 'everywhere presenting us with an overwhelming multitude of ways in which a word is written, and not unfrequently adopting the false instead of the true spelling.' The word *self* is written seolf, self, and sylf ; *we shall*, we sceolon and sculon ; *long*, lang and long ; *man*, man, man, mon ; *head*, heáuod, heáfod ; *they*, hig, hie, hí ; *dry*, dri, drig, drẏg ; *you*, geow, eow. The accent also is constantly neglected, although it is often the only clue to the meaning of the word, as ac=but, ác=an oak, is=is, ís=ice, etc. The accent generally denotes the long or broad sound of the vowels ; thus *for, fór*, should be pronounced for, fore. God=God ; gód=good, like *goad*. But the real pronunciation of Anglo-Saxon, being now a dead language, can often be only guessed at and conjectured, especially by reference to the living cognate tongues, Icelandic, Danish, German, and others.*

SAXON A SYNTHETIC LANGUAGE.

16. The grammar may be generally described as of a *synthetic* character. This will be perfectly intelligible to any one possessing the slightest knowledge of the classic tongues, but may require explanation for those that are unacquainted with any but their own. *Synthesis* (σύν *with*, θῆσις *a placing*) implies *composition*, or a putting together. Two things seem to be needed in every language in order to make complete sense : the expression of our *notions* or *ideas*, and the expression of the relation these notions bear

---

* Observe also that in some of the very oldest MSS. extant, such as the Cotton MS. used by Mr. Sweet in his new edition of Gregory's Pastorals, there seem to be no accents at all. Hence all we can say with certainty regarding them is that, though not used constantly, when they do occur they are a safe guide to the pronunciation, or at least the length of the vowel, as they appear to be scarcely ever employed incorrectly. Thus, though *ác=oak* may be found unaccented, *ac=but* will never be met with an accent.

one to another. In this respect words have been divided into two great classes, the *notional* and the *relational*. The language which fuses these two into one, and effects the purpose by a simple change or modification of the notional words, is said to be a synthetic language, and will be so to a greater or lesser extent in proportion to the use it makes of the relational (see also paragraph 92). The Anglo-Saxon makes a very considerable use of these. It is, therefore, synthetic only in a moderate degree. Consequently the changes or inflexions of its words are fewer, and its grammar much simpler, than the Latin or the Greek. As the only real difference between Anglo-Saxon and modern English consists in the almost total absence of these inflexions from the latter, a slight acquaintance with them will be necessary to understand the nature of the change.

THE DEFINITE ADJECTIVE.

17. The definite article or adjective was twofold : 1. The indeclinable, answering to our definite *the*, but used also relatively, and as a demonstrative pronoun. 2. The declinable, neutral þæt ; masculine, se ; feminine, seó, which corresponds also to the demonstrative *is, ea, id*. It is declined as follows:—

	Neut.	Mas.	Fem.			
Sing. N.	þæt	se	seó	Plur. N. A.	þá	
A.	þæt	þone	þá	D.	{ þam / þœm }	for all Genders.
Ab.	þy		þære	G.	þara	
D.		{ þám / þœm }	þære			
G.		þæs	þære			

Both of these definite particles are constantly blended together, se-þe *he who*, þætte (contracted for þæt þe) *that which*, as : ic wát þætte eall þæt ic her sprece is wi þínum willan, *I know that all that I here speak is against thy will.*

GENDER AND DECLENSION.

18. There is no fixed rule to determine the genders of the nouns. These were originally regulated, not so much by nature, as in English, as by the terminations, which were already in great part lost or confounded in the most ancient state of the language we are acquainted with. All words in *a*, however, are masculine, as *se mona*, the moon. Of declensions there are two orders, the *simple* and the *complex*. To the first are referred all nouns ending in a *radical e* for the feminine and neutral, and *a* for the masculine, which are declined in exactly the same manner, except that, as in Latin, the neuter N. and A. for both numbers is always alike. This order also includes the *definite* form of all adjectives, *i.e.* the form of the adjective, which is used when it is preceded by the definite article, any demonstrative or possessive pronoun, and the possessive case. *Simple Order* or first *Declension*.

SINGULAR.

	Neut.	*Mas.*	*Fem.*
N.	eáre (ear)	nama (name)	heorte (heart)
G. D.	eáran	naman	heortan
A.	eáre	naman	heortan

PLURAL.

	Neut.	*Mas.*	*Fem.*
N. A.	eáran	naman	heortan
D.	eárum	namum	heortum
G.	éarena	namena	heortena

So the definite adjective :—

SING.

	Neut.	*Mas.*	*Fem.*
N.	þæt swifte,	se swifta,	seo' swifte (the swift),
G. D.	swiftan,	swiftan,	swiftan,
A.	swifte,	swiftan,	swiftan.

PLUR. FOR ALL GENDERS.
N. A. þá swiftan,
D. swiftum,
G. swiftena.

It thus appears that in this order there are, in reality, not more than three inflexional forms : -*an* for all the oblique cases in the sing., and the Nom. and Acc. plural ; -*um* for the Dat. and Abl. ; and -*ena* for the Gen. plural : nama, naman, namum, namena.

ORIGIN OF THE MODERN POSSESSIVE AND PLURAL.

19. The next, or complex order, is much more intricate, comprising two distinct declensions, each varying for all the three genders. We can spare room for the masculines only of the first of these, which, of all the A.S. declensions, is the most interesting to us, as that to which all English nouns have been conformed so far as they are inflected. It is as follows :—

Sing. N. A. *weg*, a way,   Plur. N. A. *wegas*, ways,
G. *weges*, way's,   G. *wega*, ways',
D. Abl. *wege*, to and by a way.   D. Abl. *wegum*, to and by ways.

Here is the true origin of the only changes to which the English noun is subjected, and about which, simple as the matter is, so many wild theories were started, at a time when the English tongue was believed to be made up of Latin, Greek, French, some Hebrew, and a little Saxon. The plural *s* was at once referred to the French, because it happened to agree with the usage of that tongue ; and the possessive '*s* was supposed to be a contraction of *his*. It was even customary to write the word in full, thus : the king *his* name, for the king's name, in imitation of an imaginary antique state of the language. However, this theory as to the origin of the possessive in modern English is an old delusion, refuted by Alexander Hume in his treatise on English Grammar, dedicated to James I., and edited by

Wheatley in 1865. He gives two good reasons against it: 'First, *His* is the masculine gender, and this may be feminine, as, a mother's love is tender; Second, because *his* is onelie singular, and this may be plural, as, al men's vertues are not knawen.'

One might almost imagine that a similar notion had at some time prevailed in Germany, where such expressions as der König seine Krone, der Vater sein Sohn, are sometimes met with. At all events, the coincidence is curious, but cannot, of course, affect the true explanation, as above given, of the origin of the possessive and the plural in modern English. Yet it must be added that even in Layamon (1200) *his* occurs in this peculiar way : 'John his book.' The question, therefore, suggests itself whether these may not be independent collateral forms that sprang up at a very remote period during the progress of the various Teutonic languages towards analysis.

INDEFINITE ADJECTIVE.

20. Besides the definite form already explained, the adjectives have an indefinite corresponding to the complex order of nouns, but of a much simpler nature. The indefinite form of *swift* is as follows :—

	SING.			PLUR.	
Neut.	*Masc.*	*Fem.*			
N. swift,	swift,	swift,	N. A. swifte,	⎫	
A. swift,	swiftne,	swifte,	D. swiftum,	⎬ for all Genders.	
			G. swiftra.	⎭	
Ab. swifte,	⎫				
D. swiftum,	⎬	swiftre.			
G. swiftes.	⎭				

Example of the use of the definite and indefinite forms :—

a swift horse = án swift hors,
the swift horse = se swifta hors,
of swift horses = swiftra horsa,
of *the* swift horses = þara swiftena horsa.

In the same way are declined all past participles in *od* and *ed*, and the participles present, both definitively and indefinitively, with the single exception of the Gen. Plur., whose definite form is *ra* instead of *ena*, as : þára rihtwillendra for rihtwillendena, *of the upright.*

DEGREES OF COMPARISON.

21. The degrees of comparison are in *-or* and *-ost*, where it should be observed that *-or* is *always* adverbial, its definite and indefinite form being *-re*, *-ra*, *-re*. *Ost* is adverbial and indefinite, making $\begin{Bmatrix} oste\ osta\ oste \\ este\ esta\ este \end{Bmatrix}$ in the definite. Example:

Comparative :
swiftor, *more swiftly*, adv.
swiftre, swiftra, swiftre, *swifter* and *the swifter*, adj. def. and indef.

Superlative :
swiftost, *most swiftly* and *swiftest*, adv. and adj. indef.
swifteste, swiftesta, swifteste, *the swiftest*, adj. def.

Some of the irregulars in *mest* are still retained in English, as : inn, innor, innemest, *in, inner, inmost,* etc.

PRONOUNS.

22. The personal pronouns generally resemble our own, but are remarkable for having preserved in the first and second persons the only remnant of the dual form to be found in the language.

	1st Person.	2nd Person.	3rd Person.		
Sing. N.	ic (I.)	þu (thou)	N. hit (it),	he (he),	heó (she)
A.	me	þe	A. hit	hine	hí
G. D.	mín	þin	D. him	him	hire
			G. his	his	hire

Dual.	Pl.	Dual.	Pl.		
N. wit	we	git	ge	Plur. N. hí (they)	⎫ for all
A. D. unc	us	inc	eow	D. him & heom	⎬ Genders.
G. uncer	úre	incer	eower	G. hira & heora	⎭

Sylf (self) is declined both indefinitely, as : ic swerige þurh me sylfne, I swear by myself ; and definitely, as : on ðá sylfan tíd, at the same time. The demonstrative þis þes þeós (hoc, hic, hæc) makes in the plural þás and þæs, whence our two forms, *these*, *those*, with a difference of meaning. The remaining pronouns present no sort of difficulty, and are recognised at a glance, as : sum, *some*, a, *manig*, *many*, etc.

VERB.

23. While the nouns and adjectives are exceedingly rich in grammatical forms, the verb presents in this respect a marked contrast to the classic languages, having at a very remote period lost the great bulk of its inflexions. This must have occurred before the arrival of the Anglo-Saxons in England, as we find it to be the case in the other cognate languages, though not quite to the same extent. The passive voice has completely disappeared, together with all the tenses of the indicative and subjunctive modes active, except the present and imperfect. There remain but thirteen actual changes to which the verb is subjected, of which five, and in some cases six, are retained in modern English ; consequently, were it not for the irregularity of many of these forms, and their ill-defined nature, the whole verbal system could be mastered in half-an-hour's study. There are two orders of verbs, corresponding to the two orders of nouns, the simple and the complex. The first, which has been called the *weak* conjugation, is pretty much the same as our ordinary method, the past tense ending in *de* or *te*, and the past participle in *d* or *t*. The complex, or *strong* conjugation, is the source of all our so-called irregular verbs, in which the past tense is a monosyllable formed by a change of vowel, and the past participle is in *-en* or *-n*. In the strong conjugation, the verb develops, within itself, its inflexional forms, by a change of the radical vowel : *drive*, *drove*, *driven* ; in the weak it requires the aid of an additional syllable: *love, loved.* The former is most in accordance with the genius of the Teutonic tongues; the extensive adoption of the latter is a sure symptom of decay: according to it are conjugated all new and imported words, for as a rule the stock of strong verbs never is increased. Here *make* has only in appearance become strong by contraction: *made = mak-ed* from *macod.* The best test in modern English of a strong verb is the participial termination. Those in *-en* or *-n* are strong: *hide, know, speak, get,* etc. All others are *weak,* either *regular* or *irregular*: *love* is *regular; make, have, lose, irregular.* A strong verb should never be called *irregular* until it drop the final *en*: English strong verbs have this tendency: *got* for *gotten, hid* for *hidden.*

FIRST ORDER (WEAK FORM).

ic macige,	macode,	macod,
I make.	made.	made.

SECOND ORDER (STRONG FORM).

breke,	brœc,	brocen,
I break.	broke.	broken.

EXAMPLE OF FIRST ORDER.
INDICATIVE.

Present.—lufige, love.   *Past.*—lufode, loved.
        lufast, lovest.   lufodest, lovedst.
        lufað, loveth.   lufode, loved.
        lufiað ⎫
  and lufige, ⎭ we, you, they love.   lufodon, ,,

SUBJUNCTIVE.

Pres.   *Past.*
Sing. 1, 2, 3 lufige.   Sing. 1, 2, 3 lufode.
Plur. 1, 2, 3 lufion.   Plur. 1, 2, 3 lufodon.

IMPERATIVE.

Sing. 2 lufa.   Plur. 2 lufiað and lufige.

INFINITIVE.

Present—lufian = to love.
Gerund (to)—lufigenne = to love.
Act. part.—lufigende = loving.
Pass. part.—(ge)-lufod = loved.

Here the three persons pl. of the pres. ind. are alike, and the same as the pl. imperative. The three pers. pl. imperfect are also alike, and the same as those of the imperfect subjunctive. The 1st and 3rd sing. imperf. ind., and the sing. of the imperf. subj. correspond in the same way, leaving, as above stated, only thirteen actual grammatical inflexions. The present is used instead of the future, and the other nice distinctions of time were but indifferently expressed, which was one of the chief causes of the obscurity attaching to Saxon writings in general. Another undoubtedly was, not the great number of forms in the noun and adjective, but their want of variety, and their exceedingly vague and unsatisfactory character. Endings like *-orum*, *-ibus*, *-abam*, *-averunt*, in Latin, are too striking to be easily forgotten, or not to be readily recognized again. Whereas the A.S. *e* and *a*, *es* and *as*, etc., are so alike, and used for so many different cases, that confusion is often difficult to be avoided. On the whole, this language, when it began to be employed for literary purposes, was already considerably weakened, and ready to be broken up altogether on the first occasion.

GRAMMATICAL EXERCISE.

24. The following extract from Alfred's free version of Boethius' 'Consolation of Philosophy,' may help to illustrate the foregoing principles of the grammar, and to show how far it differs from modern English :—

We sculon[1]	get	of	ealdum[2]	leasum[2]	spellum[2]	þe	sum
We shall (must)	*yet (now)*	*of*	*old*	*lying*	*tales*	*to thee*	*some*

1. Scealan, to owe (defective), ic sceal, we sculon ; subj. imperf. ic sceolde, we sceoldon, implies obligation, hence its subsequent future meaning.
2. From eald (old), leas (false), and spell (a tale), *um*, universal, Dat. and Abl., Pl. for all nouns and adjectives, governed by *of*, cf, de, ex.

II.—Anglo-Saxon Period.

bispell[3] reccan.   Hit gelamp[4]   gió þætte án hearpere wœs[5]
by-tale reckon (tell).   It happened (long)   ago that a harper was

on þære[6] þeode[6] þe[7] þracia hátte.[8]   þæs[9] nama wæs[5] Orfeus.   He
in the land that Thrace hight.   His name was Orfeus.   He

hæfde[10] án swīthe œnlic[11]   wif.[11]   Seó wœs[5] háten[12]
had a very one-like (unique) wife.   She was hight

Eurydice.   Þa ongann[13] monn[14] secgan[24] be   þám[15] hearpere,[15]
Eurydice.   Then began man say by (of) the harper,

þæt he mihte[16] hearpian   þæt se wudu wagode[17] for þam swege,
that he might harp so-that the wood waved for the sound,

and wilde deor[18]   þær   woldon[19] to-irnan and standan swilce hi
and wild beasts thither would to-run and stand as if they

---

3. By-tale, or example, cf. gód-spell, good-tale, or history, hence gospel.
4. Past from gelimpan, to happen.
5. From wesan, to be; past, wæs, wære. wæs; Pl. wæron—was, were—usually called the imperfect of *to be* in our grammars!
6. Dat. sing. fem. from seo theod, the land or people, governed by *on*.
7. The indefinite article and pronoun, as explained in § 6.
8. Past of hátan, to have a name, be called—retained in old English 'Bright is her hue, and Geraldine she hight.'—*Lord Surrey.*
9. Genitive masc. of definite article of him—see § 6.
10. Past of habban, to have, ic hæfde, hæfdest, hæfde; Pl. hæfdon, had.
11. Acc. sing. neut. Were wif fem. the adj. would be in this case œnlice, indef. form, and the def. œnlican.
12. Past participle of hátan, used also in old English: 'Among the rest a good old woman was hight Mother Hubbard.'—*Spenser.*
13. Onginnan, ongan, ongunnen.
14. Used indefinitely as in German, cf. the French *on* (on dit, etc.), contr. from homme.
15. Dat. from se hearpere, governed by *be*.
16. From magan, pres. mæg, magon; imperf. mihte, mihton: may, might, in the sense of *being able*.
17. From wagian, to wag, move; imperf. ic wagode, wagodest, wagode.
18. It meant first a wild beast (cf. Greek θήρ), then *game,* and lastly

tame wæron,³ swá stille þeáh   hí menn²⁰ oððe hundes²¹ with²²
tame were,   so   still though   them men   or   hounds against

códon,²³ þæt hí   hí ná ne onscuncdon. Þa sædon²⁴ hí þæt
went, that they them not not shunned. Then said they that

þœs⁹ hearperes¹⁵ wíf sceoldé acwelan,²⁵ and hire²⁶ sawle mon¹⁴
the   harper's   wife should die,   and her   soul man

sceoldé¹ lædan to helle.²⁷
should   lead to hell.

VOCABULARY—KELTIC ELEMENT.

25. From their first landing in the island down to the Norman Conquest, that is to say, throughout the whole of the present period, the only nations the Anglo-Saxons came in contact with were the British and Irish Kelts from the beginning, the Romans at the time of their conversion, about 600 A.D., and the Northmen, who first appeared in the year 787. By none of these was the structure of the language affected in the slightest degree. How far they influenced its vocabulary remains to be seen. First Kelts.—The very faint impression made by these on the Anglo-Saxon has always been a matter of astonishment. So imperceptible,

a particular species of game. Shakspeare says: 'Rats, and mice, and other small deer.'

19. From willan: pres. ic wille, wilt, wile; imperf. wolde, woldest, wolde; plur. woldon; subj. imperf. wolde, woldon—will, would—implying determination, hence *future*.

20. Mann, gen. mannes; plur. menn for mannas—man, men.

21. This should be *hundas*, like wegas in § 8. The confusion of gen. sing. *es*, and plur. *as*, is a sure symptom of decay.

22. Cf. *withstand*, our *with* = cum is from *mid*.

23. Irreg. pres. ic. ga and gange; imperf. ic. eóde; plur. eodon; part. past gan and gangen (Scotch gang, gee, gaen).

24. Secgan: imperf. ic. sœgde and sœde; plur. sœdon—say, said.

25. Cwellan, to quell or kill.

26. See § 11.

27. Dat. sing., from Hell; gen. helles.

II.—*Anglo-Saxon Period.*

indeed, is it, that it was formerly supposed that the last comers simply rooted the aboriginal inhabitants out of the country. This solution, however, of the difficulty cannot be received without some reserve, though, were the truth known, perhaps it would be found that there was not a very great number left to be exterminated. The wars of the empire, in which the natives of Britain took such a distinguished part, now setting up one usurper and now another, the dreadful famine and pestilence of 412, the constant inroads of the Picts and Scots immediately preceding the invasion, and the horrors that attended it, must have considerably diminished the 'hominum infinita multitudo' of which Cæsar speaks, and well nigh depopulated a land known to Diodorus Siculus as the πολυάνθρωπος νῆσος. All this considered, the statement of Creasy, in his 'English Constitution,' will not appear overdrawn, 'that the Saxons almost entirely extirpated or expelled the *men* of British race, whom they found in the parts of this country which they conquered. . . . By reason of the union of the British females with the Saxon warriors, the British element was largely preserved in our nation.' But it is probable that many of the male captives, and of those who submitted, were enslaved or employed as servants of the conquerors. It is remarkable that the nature of the thirty words, or thereabouts, known to have been retained from these, shows that, whether male or female, they were reduced to a complete state of thraldom. The following list is given by Latham from Garnett with their Welsh or British equivalents :—

Welsh.	*English.*	*Welsh.*	*English.*	*Welsh.*	*English.*
basgawd,	basket.	crochan,	crockery.	mattog,	mattock.
berfa,	barrow.	crog,	crook.	mop,	mop.
botwm,	button.	cyln,	kiln.	rhail,	rail.
bran,	bran.	dantaeth,	dainty.	rhuwch,	rug.
clwt,	clout.	darn,	darn.	sawduriaw,	solder.
		fflaw,	flaw.	tacl,	tackle, &c.

LATIN ELEMENT—THE WORD CHURCH.

26. Although Britain was for nearly 400 years an integral part of the empire, the traces the Romans left behind them were only a few geographical or military names, such as *Colonia* in Lincoln (Lindi colonia), and those ending in caster, chester, cester (castra), together with the single word street=*street*, which may be questioned, as we find it current in the other kindred tongues: Danish = stræde, Dutch = straat, German = strasse, all referable to the Teutonic root of *strew*. These remains, such as they are, have been honoured with a distinct classification of their own, that of the Latin of the *first*, or *Keltic*, or *Roman Period* (Latham and others). The remains of the Latin of the *second* or *Christian* Period are more important, without being very numerous. They are such Church words as were introduced by the Roman missioners, and may be still recognized by the very English air they have now assumed. But see paragraph 97.

Saxon.	Latin.	Saxon.	Latin.
mynster,	monasterium.	portic,	porticus.
profost,	propositus.	pall,	pallium.
cluster,	claustrum.	munuc,	monachus.
calic,	calix.	candel,	candela.
bisceop,	episcopus.	sanct,	sanctus.
mœsse,	missa.	pistel,	epistola, etc.

Cyrice (church), one writer observes, is not Latin, but from the Greek κυρίου οἶκος, the house of the Lord, 'a circumstance which points out the age of Saxon Christianity as antecedent to the influence of Rome. The Eastern Church assumed this name, but the Western always used the term *ecclesia* or congregation. *Church* and *Kirk* are relics of the ancient British Christianity.' A remarkable instance of the value and power of words, if the same term *Church* could possibly be made to serve the double purpose of pointing out the source of the Saxon, and of indicating the previous existence in the island of the British Christianity! It may be well, moreover, to observe that congregations were quite as common in the East as in the West, and that without them it were hard to understand the object of building these 'houses of the Lord.' Again, ἐκκλησία is itself Greek, used in the New Testament and by the Greek Fathers in the double sense usually assigned to all these words, and notoriously to *Church*. 'The *Church* is undoubtedly one,' etc. (Archbishop Whately.) Besides, this Greek derivation of the word is doubtful, resting on the authority of Wal. Strabo (about 850): 'ab ipsis autem Græcis *Kyrch* à *Kyrios*,' etc. The theory is that the Mœso-Goths, converted by Ulphilas, about 370, took it from the Greeks, and then handed it over to the other German tribes, including the Saxons, who brought it with them to Britain. But what these pagans wanted with such terms, for centuries before their conversion, is not explained. Admitting this view, however, what becomes of 'the relics of the ancient British Christianity?' As the term has been considerably abused, and has occasioned much misconception, it was worth while examining its claims for distinction.

NORSE ELEMENT.

27. The country was infested by the Northmen from the year 787, down to the Norman invasion. The whole of East Anglia was yielded by Alfred to Godrum in 878, and a Danish dynasty ruled the land between the years 1013 and 1042. All the Northmen, whether Danes, Norwegians, or Icelanders, were of Scandinavian race, speaking, with little dialectic variety, the common Norse language. How far the Saxon was influenced by this has been matter of dispute, some going so far as to call the language in its latter state Dano-Saxon, others maintaining that 'it has not yet been clearly proved that any considerable part of the standard form of the English language is, in its origin, Scandinavian, as distinguished from Germanic' (Craik). This is the view taken by Rask, himself a Dane, who asserts emphatically, that the Danes did not corrupt the Saxon, but that 'it was the frequent expeditions of the Scandinavian nations into England, which, next to the introduction of Christianity, gave the first blow to the ancient language in the kingdoms of the north. The Danes continued their course of wars and victories the longest and most steadfastly; their language has consequently undergone the greatest changes, and from Canute's conquest of England we may date the decline of the Icelandic (Norse) in Denmark' (*Preface*). The reason of this is very obvious. The Saxon was a cultivated tongue, reduced to a fixed state, and adapted to literary purposes, while the Norse was yet without grammar or dictionary, and so unfit for composition, that Canute's laws, and all public acts, were issued in Anglo-Saxon. The Danes that settled in the country were rapidly absorbed by the Saxon element, and civilization again got the better of the rude and ignorant barbarian: 'Græcia capta ferum victorem cepit.' Indeed the slight impression left by the Danes is a singular confirmation of the prophetic words of the Venerable Archbishop of Canterbury, Elpheg, martyred in the year 1012: 'If ye (Danes) despise my counsel, know that ye shall perish, as did Sodom, and *shall not strike root in this land*.' The words actually introduced by them may be described as *geographical, proper names* and *provincial*, rather than such as enter into the current speech.

    Geographical: *by* substituted for *tun* (town) in the parts most occupied by them, as Newby for Newton, so Whitby, Grimsby, Derby, etc. A broad pronunciation of *ceaster, chester*, as Doncaster, Tadcaster, Lancaster. *Kirk* for *church*, in Scotland generally, and in Kirkby, Kirkdale, Kirkham, Ormskirk, etc. These peculiarities, wherever found, are considered as indicative of a Danish occupation. They occur most frequently in

Yorkshire and Lincoln, thence westward to the Isle of Man, and north to the Lowlands.

Proper Names: the patronymic ending *son*, substituted for the Saxon *-ing*, Edgarson for Edgaring. 'All the numerous Ander-sons, Thomp-sons, John-sons, Nel-sons, etc., are more or less Danish, as opposed to Angle' (Latham).

Provincialisms: gar = make (göra, Swedish), lile = little (lille, Danish), greet = weep (grata, Icelandic), etc.

A few common words, undoubtedly Norse, are: take, till, bask, ill, etc.

What other terms may have forced themselves into the general language it is now impossible to point out, as they seem to have at once conformed to the Saxon mode of pronunciation, as opposed to the broader Danish. Thus the northern title *iarl* becomes *eorl* (earl), whether used in the original A.S. sense of *noble*, or in the Danish sense of *governor*, *ruler*, and the Danish King *Swayn* is *Swen*, or *Swein*, in A.S. orthography.

TRACES OF DIALECT—'DANO-SAXON.'

28. The language we have been hitherto considering may be looked upon as a rude mingling of the dialects of the Saxons, Angles, Jutes or Goths, and Frisians. These appear to have very soon coalesced into one common speech, just as the tribes themselves united into one nationality. Its state before this union was effected we know nothing of, being acquainted with it only when it began to be used for literary purposes, which was about the year 600. King Ethelbert's laws, issued soon after his conversion to Christianity in 596, are, perhaps, the oldest extant specimens of A.S. From this time to the Norman Conquest, we find a fixed and regular tongue, preserving itself almost without change for nearly 500 years; nor can we discover any clear traces of dialectic variety in the literary remains of the period, except two celebrated interlinear MSS. of the Gospel, the *Rushworthian* and the *Lindisfarne*, supposed to be written in the Northumbrian dialect during the occupation of the country by the Danes. Hickes calls it the 'Dialectus Dano-Saxonica,' which is sufficiently correct as descriptive of its nature, but erroneous as used by him to imply the general state of the language prevailing at the time. The peculiar features of this Northumbrian dialect show unmistakable symptoms of approaching decay. The grammatical *inflexions* are often weakened or neglected, final consonants are dropped, as *habba* for *habban* (to have), *buta* for *butan* (without), *ilca* for *ilcan* (the same). The genders are confused, and the rules of construction much simplified. Many of these peculiarities may be safely ascribed to the Angles, who seated themselves in Northumberland, and who probably derived them from their Scandinavian neighbours previous to their arrival in England.

POETIC SYSTEM—LAWS OF ALLITERATION.

29. It is now certain that Turner was mistaken, when he asserted that A.S. versification 'had really no other rule than the poet's ear,' and elsewhere says it differed from prose only by a more stately diction and pomp of words; for Rask has shown that it has, in common with the other kindred tongues, especially Icelandic, a fixed structure, the most striking feature of which is *alliteration*, or head-rhyme, just as the syllabic quantity may be said to distinguish the classic, and end-rhyme combined with accent, the modern system. Accent, however, is quite as essential to A.S. verse as it is to English, the alliteration itself being, in fact, regulated by it. The lines are always arranged in couplets, grouped not according to sense, but to the alliteration, which requires that two *accented syllables* in the first, and one in the second line, begin with the *same* letter if a consonant, with a *different*, if possible, when a vowel. These three initial letters are called *rhyming letters*, the third, standing in the second line, being the *chief letter*, according to which the two of the previous verse must be regulated. These are, therefore, called *sub-letters*. In the couplet there should not be more than three *accented* syllables beginning with this letter, and the *chief letter* must begin the first *accented* syllable or word of the second line. Finally, in *very short* verse, and especially when the *rhyming letters* are double, *sc, st, sw, dr, gr*, etc., there need be but *one sub-letter*. This is the doctrine of alliteration, or head-rhyme, invariably observed in A.S. poetry, as laid down by Rask. He gives the following example from Beowulf, 1108:—

1	{ In *C*áines *c*ynne	In Cain's kin
	Þone *c*weal gewræc	The murder avenged
2	{ E*c*e drihten,	The Eternal Lord,
	þoes þe he *A*bel slóg :	Because he slew Abel :
3	{ Ne ge*f*eah he þære *f*œhðe,	He got no joy from his hatred,
	Ac he hine *f*éor for*w*ræc,	But He, the Creator, drove him
4	{ *M*étod for þý *m*áne	For that misdeed,
	*M*áncynne fram.	Far from the human race.

In couplet 1 the rhyming letter is *c*, found twice in the first and once in the second line. It is arranged not according to the sense, but to the laws of alliteration. In 2 there are only two rhyming vowels, which, according to rule, are different, *e* and *a*. None of the words preceding *Abel* are *accented*, as required ; *f* is the rhyming letter in 3, where the *f* of *ge-feah* is the first letter of the *accented* syllable, *ge* being an unaccented prefix. The fourth *f* (in *forwræc*) begins an unaccented syllable ; *for* is, therefore, no violation of the law, which requires that not more than *three accented syllables* begin with the rhyming letter. In 4 the *m* is quite regular.

RHYME—ITS PROBABLE ORIGIN.

30. Besides this, there are evident traces of *end* or *final-rhyme*, which Rask thinks was employed by the northerns

from a very remote period, though there is only one A.S. poem extant, known as the 'rhyming poem,' in which it is used throughout. In Latin poetry it is employed very freely, especially by St. Aldhelm, the first Saxon who wrote Latin verse. He was educated at Malmesbury, by Mailduff, an Irishman, under whom 'he became thoroughly versed in Latin and Greek' (Turner). From this and other circumstances it is highly probable that the A.S. adopted endrhyme from the Irish, who are believed to be the first that introduced the practice into Latin poetry. At least, it is certain that the most ancient extant specimens of Latin rhyme are the compositions of Irishmen and their disciples. A proof of this is the very old hymn of St. Fechin, who flourished about 570:—

> De hinc fuit monachorum
> Dux et Pater tercentorum
> Quos instruxit lege morum
> Murus contra vitia.—Amen.

SPECIMENS OF SAXON PROSE AND VERSE.

31. 'Saxon literature,' Dr. Lingard writes, 'comprised only a few national poems and books of devotion: the treasures of history and science were still locked up in the obscurity of a learned tongue' (I. IV.). The general literary language, such as we are acquainted with, is supposed to be southern or Saxon, rather than northern or Angle. The political supremacy of Wessex, and the influence of Alfred, a native of Berkshire, may have caused it to become the ruling speech, and the standard literary model, just as the writings of Dante, Boccaccio, and Petrarch elevated the local *Tuscan* dialect into the classic *Italian*. Some have even asserted that all works, in whatever form originally composed, were subsequently conformed to the genius of the speech rendered classic by Alfred. This would certainly account for the few traces of local peculiarities deviating from those of Wessex in the literary remains which have reached us. A few specimens selected from writers of various periods will be sufficient to show the great uniformity of the language throughout.

CÆDMON, DIED ABOUT 680.

The compositions attributed to this first and greatest of A.S. poets, would fill altogether a book about the size of half *Paradise Lost.* The greater portion of them are, unquestionably, spurious.* Here is a fragment of his referred to by Bede, IV. 24, and preserved in Alfred's Anglo-Saxon version of Bede's work. It is universally allowed to be genuine :—

nu we sceolon herigean	now we shall praise
heofon-rices weard,	heaven-kingdom's guard
metodes mihte	the Creator's might
and his mód-ge-þanc	and his mind-thought
weorc wuldor-fœdor,	work's glory-father
swa he wundra gehwœs	how he of wonders
éce drihten	eternal Lord
ord onstealde.	the beginning formed.
He œrest scóp	He first shaped
eorðan bearnum	the earth for the children (of men)
heofon tó hrófe	heaven as a roof
hálig scippend	the holy Creator
ðá middangeard	then the mid-world
modcynnes weard,	mankind's guard
éce drihten	eternal Lord
æfter teóde,	afterwards made
firum foldan	for men the earth
freá ælmihtig.	Lord Almighty.

---

* 'The poem as it now exists has, probably, been materially altered by the reciters and transcribers of a later period. It has been twice published, first by Francis Junius in 1655, and next by Mr. Benj. Thorpe in 1832' [also by C. W. M. Grein in 1857]. Preface to Forshall and Madden's 'Wycliffite Versions of Holy Writ,' 1850.

George Stephens mentions a MS. of this fragment. C.C.C., Oxford, about the tenth century, which, he says, is the oldest of all, and written in the original Northumbrian dialect very soon after Bede's death, 'The Ruthwell Cross, London and Copenhagen, 1866,' p. 32. I have not had an opportunity of seeing this MS., nor am I aware that it has ever been published; but if it corresponds with this description, it certainly deserves to be more generally known. It might help, perhaps, to throw some further light on the Northumbrian dialect, the true nature of which is still but partly understood.

ALFRED, 850–900

(From the Preface to his version of St. Gregory's Pastoral, explaining the object of such versions generally).

Ic wundrode swidhe þæra godera witena þe geo wæron
I wondered much of the good wise-men that long ago were

geond Angelcyn and þa béc befullan ealle geleornod hæfdon
through (in) England and the books fully all learned had

þæt hira þa nanne dael noldon on hira agen ge þeode
that of-them no part not-would into their own native speech

wendan, ac ic þa sona eft me sylfum andwyrde and cwæð,
turn, but I then soon after to-myself answered and said,

hí ne wendon þoet æfre men sceoldon swa recelease wurðan
they (did) not think that ever men should so careless become

and seo lar swa ðofeallan. . . . For þi me þingð betere gif
and the lore so fall-off. . . . Wherefore me thinks better if

geow swa þincð þæt we eac sume béc þa þemed heþyrfysta
you so think that we also some books that seem most-needed

syn eallum mannum to witanne þæt we þa on þæt
be to all men to understand that we them into that

ge-þeode wendon þe we ealle ge-cnawan mægen, and ge-don swa
speech turn that we all know may, and cause, as

we swiðe eaðe magon mid Godes fultume þæt eall seo geoguð
we very easily may with. God's help, that all the youth

þe nu is on Angel-cynne freora manna þara þe þa speda
that now is in England of-free men of those that the wealth

hæbben, þæt hi þam befeollan mægen syn to leornunge
have   that they themselves support,   may into learning

oðfaeste þa hwile þe hí nanre oðre note ne mægen, oð
be-put   the while that they to no other things not may, till

fyrst þe hí wel cunnen Englisc geurit arædan.
first that they well can   English writing read.

ÆLFRIC, DIED 1006

(De Veteri Testamento).

Ða   næfde he nan setl hwær he sittan mihte, forðanðe nan
Then not-had he no seat where he sit might, for that no

heofon nolde hine aberan, ne nan rice   næs þe his
heaven not-would him bear,   nor no kingdom not-was that his

mihte beon ongean Godes willan þe geworhte ealle ðinc, etc.
might be against God's will that wrought all things, etc.

SAXON CHRONICLE FOR THE YEAR 1087

(Death of William the Conqueror).

He swealt on Normandige on þone næxtan dæg æfter Nativitas
He died   in Normandy on the   next day after the Nativity

Sce Marie; and man begyrgede hine on Cathum æt Sce Stephanes
of St. Mary; and man buried   him in Caen at St. Stephen's

mynstere. . . . Gif hwa gewilniged to gewitane hu gedon man he
minster. . . . If who   wish   to   know   how to-do man he

was, oððe hwilcne wurðscipe he hæfde, oððe hu fela lande
was, or what   worship he had,   or of-how many lands

he wære hlaford, þonne wille we of him awritan swa swa we hine
he was lord, then   will we of him write   so as we him

ageaton: we him onlocodan, and oððre hwile on his hirede
knew: we him on-looked, and other while in his household

wunedon.
dwelt.

This portion of the Saxon Chronicle (1034-1087) has been attributed to Wulfstan, Bishop of Worcester, who was born in 1007, and died in 1095. If to these few names we add those of another Wulfstan, Archbishop of York (1003-1023), author of some pastorals and sermons; Cynewulf, Bishop of Winchester; the Abbot Alfric, and some national poems and songs, such as the Beowulf, the Judith, the Battle of Finsburgh, &c., by unknown writers, we shall have well-nigh exhausted the list of names that occur in A.S. literature.

Ælfric, the Archbishop, translated the first seven books of the Bible into very simple Saxon, carefully avoiding the use of all obscure words, in order, as he himself tells us, to be understood by the most illiterate, and to render the Scriptures familiar to all classes, anticipating Wickliff by, at least, 470 years. Other portions of it, especially the N.T., had been translated much earlier.

The subjoined extracts from the Gospel of St. Mark (I. 1-6), in the West Saxon and Northumbrian versions, will serve to illustrate the difference between the Northern and Southern dialects, and between each of these at various periods. The first is from the Corpus MS., Cambridge, written 'in Monasterio Baðþonio,' by a certain Ælfric, about the year 1000. The second, which seems to be a later copy of the same, say about 1050, is from the Hatton MS., Oxford. Both of these are in the Southern dialect. The third is from the famous Lindisfarne MS., also known as the 'Durham Book' (Cotton, Nero, D. 4), the Latin text of which was written by Eadfrith, Bishop of Lindisfarne, about the year 700, and the Anglo-Saxon gloss by Aldred, a priest, some 250 years later. The fourth is from the Rushworth MS., a copy of the foregoing, made about 750, and the gloss about 975. These two are in the Northumbrian, which has been called the 'Dano-Saxon' dialect (see § 28). They are all taken from Skeat's synoptical edition, Cambridge and London, 1871. Nos. III. and IV. are the only extant remains of the Anglian of the North as opposed to the Saxon of the South. The missing words in these two

II.—Anglo-Saxon Period.

glosses I have supplied, between brackets, from No. I., of which also the English is a *verbatim* version.

I. 1. Her is godspellys angyn hælyndes cristes godes suna.
II. 1. Her ys godspelles angin hælendes cristes godes sune.
III. 1. Fruma godspelles hælendes crist sunu godes.
IV. 1. On fruma godspelles hælendes cristes sunu godes.
Here is gospel's beginning of the healing Christ God's son.

I. 2. Swa awriten is on þæs witegan béc isaiam. nu ic
II. 2. Swa awritan ys on þas witegen bæch ysaiam. nu ic
III. 2. Suæ awritten is in esaia ðone witgo. heonu
IV. 2. Swa awriten is in esaia þone witgu. henu
2. *As written is in the prophet's book Isaia. now I*

I. asende minne engel be-foran þinre asyne. Se
II. asænde minne ængel beforan þinre ansiene. Se
III. [ic asende] engel min befora onsione þin. Seðe
IV. ic sende engel min beforan onseone þine. Seþe
send my angel before thy face. he

I. ge-gearwiað þinne weg be-foran ðe. 3. Clypiend
II. ge-gærewed þinne weig be-foren þe. 3. Clepiende
III. foregearuas wege ðin [be-foran ðe]. 3. Stefn
IV. foregearwað weg þinre [beforan ðe]. 3. Stemn
prepares thy way before thee. 3. *A crying*

I. stefn on þam westene ge-gearwiað drihtenes weg
II. stefne on þam westene, ge-gærewied drihtnes weig
III. cliopendes in woestern gearuas woeg drihtnes
IV. cliopande in westenne gearwigað weig drihtnes
voice in the waste get ready the Lord's way

I. doð rihte his siðas.   4. Johannes wæs on westene
II. doð rihte his syðas.   4. Johannes wæs on wœstene
III. rehta doeð stiga his.   4. wæs iohannes in woestern
IV. rehte doað stige his.   4. wæs iohannes in westenne
do (make) right his steps. 4. *John was in the waste*

I. fulligende and bodiende dædbote fulwiht on
II. fulgende and bodiende deadbote fulluht on
III. gefulwade and bodade fulwiht hreownisses on
IV. gefulwade and bodade fullwiht hreownisse in
baptizing and preaching of repentance the baptism in

Specimens of Saxon Prose and Verse. 43

I.	synna forgyfenesse.	5. And to him ferde ealle
II.	senne forgyfenysse.	5. And to hym ferde ealle
III.	forgefnisse synna.	5. And foerende woes to him
IV.	forgefnisse synna.	5. And fœrende wæs to him
	sins' forgiveness.	5. *And to him fared all*

I.	hierosolima-ware and wæron fram him gefullode
II.	ierosolima-ware and wæren fram him gefullode
III.	ða hierusolomisco waras alle and weoron gefulwad
IV.	ð hierosolimisc [ware] aalle and [wæron] gefullwade
	Jerusalem-men and were from him baptized

I.	on iordanes flode hyra synna anddetenne. 6. And
II.	on iordanes flode heore synna andettenne. 6. And
III.	fram him in iordanes stream ondetende synno hiora. 6. And
IV.	from him in iordanes streame ondetende synna heora. 6. And
	in Jordan's flood their sins confessing. 6. *And*

I.	iohannes wæs gescryd mid oluendes hærum
II.	iohannes wæs ge-scryd mid olfendes hære
III.	wæs iohannes gegerelad mið herum camelles
IV.	wæs iohannes gegerelad mið herum cameles
	John was shrouded with camels' hair

I.	and fellen gyrdel wæs ymbe his lendenu
II.	and fellen gyrdel wæs embe his lendene
III.	and gyrdils fellera ymb sido his
IV.	and gyrdels fellenne ymb lendenu his
	and a skin's girdle was about his loins

I.	and gærstapan and wudu hunig he æt,
II.	and garstapen and wude hunig he æt,
III.	and lopestro and wudu hunig . . . wæsl-gebrec.
IV.	and waldstapan and wudu huniges . . . brucende wæs.
	and locusts and wood honey he ate.

QUESTIONS.

12. What are the natural stages of the English language? How may they be designated? Explain their nature. How is the middle period subdivided? Give the names and dates of these five periods.

13. What importance do you attach to a slight knowledge of the language during the first period? How far does the alphabet differ

II.—*Anglo-Saxon Period.*

from the Latin? It possessed two peculiar letters not now used. Why is this to be regretted? Account for their disappearance.

14. There is both *reason* and *authority* for believing that the A.S. borrowed this alphabet from the Irish, rather than the Irish from them?

15. What was the state of the orthography? How was the accent employed?

16. Describe the general nature of the grammar. What are *notional* and *relational* words?

17. How many definite adjectives? These were used in a variety of ways? Origin of our article *the*?

18. How was gender determined? How many orders of declension? In the first, how many actual inflexions?

19. In the second, which form is most important to us? Why?

20. The adjective had two forms? How used? How was the definite form declined? The indefinite?

21. The degrees of comparison were double? The difference between *swiftor* and *swiftra*?

22. Which of the personal pronouns possessed a dual form? What case is *him*? Genitive of *hit*? Origin of the words *these*, *those*?

23. There is a marked difference between the state of the nouns and verbs? How many possible changes is an A.S. verb liable to? How many of these are retained in the English verb? What is meant by a *weak* and a *strong* conjugation? Distinguish an irregular from a *strong* verb in *English*.

25. The number and *nature* of Keltic words introduced at this period? What is the historical importance of these words?

26. Two classes of Latin words? The word *church* has given occasion to a theory which does not seem tenable?

27. To what race did the Northmen belong? What does Rask say about their influence on the A.S. language? What sort of words did they introduce? Why is it difficult to say whether a word is Danish or Saxon in its origin?

28. There are proofs of the existence of *one dialect* at this period. What is its nature?

29. The chief characteristic of A.S versification? What were its laws? Show that *accent* was essential?

30. To what extent was *end-rhyme* employed? Its probable origin?

31. Mention the principal names that occur in A.S. literature. Account for the great uniformity of the written language throughout this period.

SECTION III.

BROKEN SAXON PERIOD (1066-1200).

BROKEN SAXON PERIOD ONE OF DISSOLUTION—TIME WHEN DECAY FIRST SET IN—ITS CAUSE—MISTAKEN VIEWS ON THIS SUBJECT—GRAMMAR BROKEN, OR UNGRAMMATICAL SAXON—VOCABULARY—SPECIMENS.

THE BROKEN SAXON PERIOD—DATES.

32. The middle or transition state of the language may be said, roughly, to extend from the arrival of the Normans to the reign of Henry VI., or to lie between the years 1066 and 1450. Before this epoch, we have seen that the language was pure Anglo-Saxon; after it we shall see that it is good modern English. But as, to get from the former to the latter, it was necessary first to break down, and then to build up again, so there are two natural subdivisions of the transition period, one of *dissolution*, and one of *reconstruction*. The first of these embraces all the time during which the old language was undergoing a process of 'disorganization and decay, without exhibiting any symptoms which the most intelligent observer could, at the time, have interpreted as presaging a return to completeness and consistency—a period of confusion, alike perplexing to those who then used the tongue, and to those who now endeavour to trace its vicissitudes.'—*Spalding*. It is usually called the *Broken Saxon* period, and various dates have been assigned for its actual duration. We have made it extend over a space of 150 years, from 1066 to 1200, which falls short of what is generally allowed to it by about half a century. Sir F. Madden closes it in 1230, Craik protracts it to 1250,

and others still further. But as, after Layamon, we have no extant Saxon in any shape, and his writings are universally referred to about 1200, the Broken Saxon state of the language seems, very naturally, to end at this time.

TWO LANGUAGES—THE WRITTEN AND SPOKEN.

33. Did it begin in 1066, or, in other words, were the first symptoms of corruption coincident with the arrival of the Normans? So far as the *written* language is concerned, the answer must be *no*. Very good A.S. was written for at least fifty years after that event. Wulfstan, Bishop of Worcester, died in 1095, and his works are grammatically correct. Such are the portions of the 'Saxon Chronicle' attributed to him, an extract from which, for the year 1087, may be seen amongst the specimens of the last section. But with the spoken language the case was very different. Craik has gone far to show that there existed, much earlier than is commonly supposed, a colloquial form of speech, side by side with the written, and resembling the more recent language in its general structure. 'The same thing seems to have taken place as in France, and other continental countries, when the Latin first became corrupted into the *Romana Rustica;* the former long continued to be the language of writing, and probably even of the educated classes in oral communication, while the latter was the popular speech, from which it gradually rose to be the dialect first of popular, then of all literature. So in this country there was probably in use a sort of English, or Broken Saxon, even in the Saxon times; and the two forms of the language, the regular and the irregular, the learned and the vulgar, the old and the new, the mother and the daughter, seem to have maintained a rivalry for, perhaps, a century or two, till the rude vigour, the rough and ready character of the one prevailed, in a time of much ignorance and general convulsion and change, over the refinement and comparative difficulty of the other' (I. 205). The earliest extant specimen of such a popular form of speech is the 'Song of Canute,' recorded by Thomas, Monk of Ely,* about 1166, 150 years after it was supposed to have been composed :—

'Merie sungen ðe muneches binnen Ely,	'Merrily sung the monks within Ely,
Tha Cnut Ching rew there by :	When that Cnut King rowed thereby :
Roweð, cnihtes, noer ðe land,	Row, knights, near the land,
And here we ðes muneches saeng.'	And hear we these monks sing.'

But these verses have such a very modern air, that although Craik thinks the words cannot be much altered from the time they were sung, it is probable that they were considerably modified in more recent MSS. from the time they were reported.

VARIOUS THEORIES TO ACCOUNT FOR THE CORRUPTION OF A.S.

34. However, if such a popular dialect did exist so early as is here implied, it will go far to account for the cause of the general decay of the language, about which so many theories have been started. It will be sufficient to mention three of these. They may be termed, for brevity sake, the

* 'Canute, going by boat to keep at Ely the feast of the Purification of the Virgin, looked up at the church that rose from a rock near the Ouse, and ordered the rowers to row slowly towards the land, that he might hear the psalms of the monks. Then calling his companions about him, he bade them sing with him, and expressing with his own mouth the gladness of his heart, composed this little song in English : —"Merie," &c., with other words which follow, still publicly sung and remembered in preverbs.' 'Historia Ecclesiæ Eliensis,' ch. 15, in vol. iii. of Dean Gale's 'Hist. Brit. Sax. Anglo-Danicæ Scriptores XV. ex vetustis MSS. editi.' Thomas tells us that he lived after A. 1166.

III.—*Broken Saxon Period.*

(*a*) Norman,
(*b*) Anti-Norman,
(*c*) Middle Course.

(*a*) According to the Norman view of the case, the change was due solely to the Conquest. That event introduced the French language, by the direct action of which upon the A.S., the corruption was brought about, which resulted in modern English. This theory may be looked upon as now out of date, and safely set aside. We shall see that the French tongue never at any time affected the *structure* of the language, and had no perceptible influence of any sort on it during the present period, the very time when the dissolution was accomplished. (*b*) The Anti-Normans run into the opposite extreme, and assert that the great event just alluded to had nothing to do with the decay. In fact, had the Normans never made their appearance, or had Harold triumphed at Hastings, the language would have lost its grammatical inflexions all the same, and would have become what it now substantially is. The only difference would have been in the vocabulary, which would have presented a more homogeneous character, possessing fewer Latin and French words. Here there is a great deal of truth, perhaps a little exaggeration. It does seem going too far to deny all connection between the dissolution of the language and the Norman Conquest. Surely the one must have hastened the other, and acted indirectly upon the A.S. in a variety of ways. Consequently it will be safer to adopt the *middle course* (*c*), which maintains, 1st, that the general corruption of the language took place, *independently* of the Norman Conquest, in accordance with a tendency inherent in all *synthetic* tongues, gradually to lose their complex grammatical system, and so become, to a greater or less extent, analytical; 2nd, that so far as the A.S. is concerned, this tendency was precipitated by the Conquest, and partly directed, or influenced, by contact with the French language.

35. An *analytic* form of speech is the reverse of the *synthetic*. It expresses by separate words, or particles, those relations of ideas to ideas, which we have seen conveyed by a change or modification of the *notional* words in the latter. A pure analytic language will possess no grammatical inflexions; a pure synthetic, no *relational* words. An example of each system will make this clear. The Chinese is nearly a perfect instance of the one, the American tongues generally of the other. In Chinese the slightest shade of meaning requires at once a separate word. Thus *day=je*, but *daily=je yung=*day use—*i. e.*, what is used or needed every day. In Aztec or Mexican, not only are ideas and their relations, but even whole idioms, thrown into one word by a sort of agglutination, which to us seems quite incomprehensible. The word notlazomahuizteopixcatatzin is explained to mean my-beloved-honoured-reveredpriestly-father. When taken to pieces, we find it made up of the following component parts: no=my+tlazotli=beloved+mahuitztic=honoured+teopixqui (from Teotl=God, and pia=to keep or guard)=priestly+tatli=father+tzin =a reverential termination (Hervas, 'Idea dell' Universo,' XVIII.). The great majority of known languages lies between these two extremes, that is to say, they are only to a certain extent either synthetic or analytic. Much has been written on the rival claims of these systems as to priority in point of time. Was speech originally void of grammar, or gifted from the first with a highly complicated structure? There does appear to be a universal law pervading all speech, in virtue of which it ever tends to change from one state to the other with equal readiness, from the simple and unartificial to the compound, and back again, ever putting together and taking asunder. The farther back we go, the more developed and elaborate do we find the inflexion state of most languages. It has thence been perhaps too hastily concluded, that this was their original condition. It may be that we do not go back far enough, and that, could we trace them to their first state, we would find that this very inflexional system, however complex it may now appear, developed itself gradually out of a simple beginning, in accordance with certain hidden laws of euphony and harmony. Indeed, the acquisition, or growth of inflexion, so far from being 'probably unknown as an actual phenomenon' (*Craik*), is demonstrated by the history of most languages, which evidently show a gradual progress from rude beginnings to a more perfect state. Little *significative* words were at first tacked on loosely to the end of roots, and then blended so with them, as in course of time to lose all independent meaning. The ending *ivus*, in Latin, is a corruption of *vis*, cf. *dat-ivus = dandi vis*. Hence its universal *active* power. The English language, were it not fixed by *writing* (an influence not brought to bear on speech in its earlier stages), would very rapidly run into a synthetic state, which, when it came to be reduced to writing, would be found of a most intricate nature. We should have, by *analogy* from *don't, won't, can't, shan't;* such forms as ain't=ought not, maún't= must not, haún't=have not. Here are already the germs of, perhaps, three negative conjugations in ó, á, and aú. Then the pronouns would quickly blend with the verb, as, in fact, they now do in speaking, developing regular tense-endings, such as: cham=I am; chav=I have; thart=thou art; thast=thou hast; hes=he is; has=he has, etc., in the Barony of Forth dialect. In this very way we know that the Indo-European verb was formed. In a word, the method pursued in the modern science of philology is based upon the supposition that language was originally analytic, consisting of roots only, chiefly monosyllabic, and gradually developing itself on synthetic principles, with a general tendency to fall back again into its primitive state.

DOWNWARD TENDENCY OF A.S.

36. A.S. formed no exception to the universal rule. A glance at the state of its grammar is sufficient to convince us that, at the time it began to be cultivated, it had already lost a great deal of its synthetic character. This is confirmed by reference to the Mœso-Gothic, Norse, and other kindred tongues, where we find a multiplicity of inflexions, especially verbal, which must have existed in the Saxon at some remote period, but which had already disappeared when the language began to be reduced to a written form. Even this written form was not strictly adhered to in the Dano-Saxon, or Northumbrian dialect, explained in the last section. This again was still further disregarded in the current popular speech long before it ceased to be employed in literature. But it has been shown that, on account of some mysterious law of consistency or analogy, all speech tends to work out within itself, and independently of all external influence, any tendency that may have once set in, either towards composition, if simple, or towards disorganization, if complex. We may, therefore, safely conclude, that as the bent of the A.S., long previous to the arrival of the Normans, was downwards towards decomposition, it would have developed this inclination to its legitimate consequences, and resulted in a form of speech *essentially* the same as the present English, independently of the Norman Conquest.

NORMAN INFLUENCE.

37. So far, then, theory (*b*) is right. But it is in vain to deny that the Invasion had anything to do with the rapid breaking up of the Saxon, which was apparent very soon after that event. Writing is, avowedly, that which exercises the most powerful influence on language in a *conservative* sense. It will stay a downward, or arrest an upward tendency. It will preserve the Greek, in a highly inflexional state, throughout ages of social and political convulsion. It will, on the other hand, prevent the Chinese from ever assuming a composite character. We believe that the art of writing was known to the Chinese at a period so very remote, that the language was still in its primitive simple condition, and that it was their literature which retained it from time immemorial in that state, stagnant, so to say, and petrified, like everything else connected with that remarkable people. The Normans virtually put an end to the Saxon literature. The only important native remains we possess, for nearly two hundred years after their arrival, are the latter portions of the 'Saxon Chronicle,' and Layamon's 'Brute.' They persecuted and trampled upon the national speech in every possible way. It was ignored by the aristocracy, excluded from all polite society, shut out even from the High Church. Wulfstan, Bishop of Worcester, was deposed, because he was 'a superannuated English idiot, who could not speak French.'—*Matt. Paris.* The laws were administered in French. In the King's court the president and chief assessors were Normans. 'Ipsum etiam idioma tantum abhorrebant, quod leges terræ, statutaque Anglorum regum lingua Gallica tractarentur, et pueris etiam in scholis principia literarum grammatica Gallice et non Anglice traderentur.'—*Ingulf*, 71, 88. The consequent neglect into which A.S. fell was, of itself, sufficient not only to hasten its decay, but even to cause it to disappear altogether in course of time, had that neglect continued.

INFLUENCE OF THE MONKS.

38. One would suppose that these potent influences, external and internal, were quite sufficient to account for the corruption. And, indeed, such was the common belief, until Mr. Guest, in his English Rhythms, discovered another,

which is worth considering. He tells us that 'the language
of our earlier literature fell at last a victim not to the Norman Conquest, for it survived that event at least a century;
not to the foreign jargon, which the weak but well-meaning Edward (the Confessor) first brought into the country,
for French did not mix with our language till the days of
Chaucer; it fell from the same deep and mighty influences
which swept every living language from the literature of
Europe. When the South regained its ascendancy, and
Rome once more seized the wealth of vassal provinces, its
favourite priests had neither the knowledge requisite to
understand, nor tastes fitted to enjoy, the literature of the
countries into which they were promoted. The road to
their favour and their patronage lay elsewhere; and the
monk, giving up his mother tongue as worthless, began to
pride himself only upon his Latinity. The legends of his
patron saint he Latinized; the story of his monastery he
Latinized; in Latin he wrote history; in Latin he wrote
satires and romances. Amid these labours he had little
time to study the niceties of A.S. grammar; and the Homilies, the English Scriptures, Cædmon's Paraphrase, the
national songs, the magnificent Iudith, and other treasures
of native genius, must soon have lain on the shelves of his
cloister as little read, or, if read, almost as little understood,
as if they had been written in a foreign tongue. When he
addressed himself to the unlearned, noble or ignoble, he
used the vulgar dialect of his shire, with its idioms, which
the written dialect had probably rejected as wanting in precision, and with its corrupt pronunciation, which alone would
require new forms of grammar.' These are the returns
made to men, without whom no English would be, perhaps,
spoken at the present day, men who alone cultivated the
language, and endeavoured to keep it together as long as
possible, toiling night and day at their dreary and thankless
task, who are the only links that connect the present with
the past here as in all other things. They first taught the

Saxons the use of letters, and created their literature, thus preserving the language in a state which enabled it to come out with comparative success from its severe struggle for ascendancy with its Norman rival. Assuredly, had not the A.S. been converted, and acquired sufficient knowledge to reduce their tongue to a written form, it would have arrived at such a stage of decomposition at the time of the invasion as would have caused it to fare no better, in face of a cultivated language, than did the Dane, the Frankish, and Longobard, under similar circumstances (see section IV. § 49).

THE GRAMMAR OF THIS PERIOD—VERB.

39. The main difference between the grammar of this period and the previous has already been partly explained. It may be generally described as *broken, ungrammatical*, or simply *bad* Saxon, as we now say *bad grammar*. If that was inflected, this is so to a less degree. The inflexions were then fixed and regulated by certain laws; they are now vague, undetermined, arbitrary, their greater or less consistency depending upon the amount of knowledge possessed by the individual writer. Hence the structure of one work will vary from that of another, though contemporary, or almost so, agreeing, however, in the chief features. Such is the relation the two most important extant compilations of the time bear to each other. These are, as already stated, the remaining portions of the Saxon Chronicle, 1100-1154, and Layamon's translation, or rather amplified imitation, of Wace's 'Brute,' 1200. Without entering into a minute analysis of the special niceties that distinguished the latter from the former, it may be sufficient to state, in a general way, that Layamon's language is considerably more corrupt than that of the 'Chronicle,' but not more so, if so much, than would be warranted by the difference of time. In contrasting this broken state of the speech with the preceding, it is obvious that the greatest change will be perceptible in the noun and adjective, the least in the verb. The verb could lose thirteen inflexions only. It actually lost but one of these, the gerund in -*nne*, or -*ne*, or rather confounded it with the present participle -*nde*=*ing*; and with the infinitive, *tó lufigenne* becoming *tó lufian*. Some of the other terminations, however, were considerably *weakened*, by the substitution of *e* for *a*, *en* for *on*, and by the occasional omission of some final letters. We have *ic macod*, and *ic maked*, for *ic macode*; *finden* for *findan*, *pene* for *pence*, *segen* for *seegan*, etc.

NOUN—POSSESSIVE AND PLURAL.

40. In the *nouns*, besides a general disregard for the proper case-endings, there is a decided preference shown for the masculine declension in *es*, gen. sing., and *as*, nom. plur., explained in the last section. According to this are declined nouns of both orders and of all genders, and even here the plur. *as* is softened into *es*, and the dative plur. in -*um* is constantly ignored. So we find *endes* for both *endas* and *endum*, *dæies* for *dæges*, *dægas*, *dægum*. The adoption of this form seems to have been due to its greater facility, rather than to any *indirect* action of the French language, requiring the Saxon to accommodate its grammar to the genius of the foreign words that began now to work their way into it. In confirmation of this latter view, Dr. Trench, in his 'English Past and Present,' cites an otherwise instructive passage from J. Grimm : 'When the English language was inundated by a vast influx of French words, few, if any, French forms were received into its grammar ; but the Saxon forms soon dropped away, because they did not suit the new roots ; and the genius of the language, from having to deal with the newly-imported words in a rude state, was induced to neglect the inflexions of the native ones. This, for instance, led to the introduction of the *s* as the universal termination of all plural nouns, which agreed with the usage of the French language, and was not alien from that of the Saxon, but was merely an extension of the termination of the ancient masculine to other classes of nouns.' Here it should be observed that this practice was followed long before any such *inundation* of French words as is here alluded to had yet set in. It was not, therefore, adopted to meet the exigencies of that language, which was probably unknown to, certainly not countenanced by, the few native writers who still adhered to the national idiom. So that the law of all composite languages, laid down by Trench himself, is not violated in this instance. 'However composite they may be, yet they are only so in regard of their words. There may be a medley in respect of these, some coming from one quarter, some from another; but there is never a *mixture* of *ungrammatical* forms and inflexions. One or other language *entirely* predominates here, and everything has to conform and subordinate itself to the laws of this ruling and ascendant language. The A.S. is the ruling language in our present English; while that has thought good to drop its genders, even so the French substantives which came among us must also leave theirs behind them, as in like manner the verbs must renounce their own conjugations, and adapt themselves to ours. 'Coeunt quidem paullatim in novum corpus peregrina vocabula, sed grammatica linguarum, unde petita sunt, ratio perit.'—W. Schlegel, p. 25-26.

ADJECTIVE—GENDER—PRONOUN.

41. With regard to the adjectives, all distinction was at once lost between the *definite* and the *indefinite* form. *The* good man, and *a* good man, would both be þe *gód* man, án *gód* man, instead of se *góda* man, án *gód* man. Their declensions were also confounded in much the same way as were those of the nouns, often disappearing altogether.

Gender, hitherto regulated according to *termination*, but always difficult and uncertain, could no longer be adhered to when the endings began to get confused. Hence the modern principle of following nature—a very simple and obvious remedy, commended by truth and common sense—began to prevail very generally.

The declinable adjective þæt, se, seó was quite superfluous by the side of the indeclinable þe=the, often used instead of it, even by the best A.S. writers.

The most striking change in the pronouns is the substitution of the dative *him* for the accusative *hine*. The modern *him* is a dative form, with an acc., and occasionally a dat. force: give him, etc.

The proper government of prepositions is not attended to: *mid cágan* for *mid cágum*, as if a Roman were to write *cum oculi*, instead of *cum oculis*.

These, and whatever further changes occurred, may be rendered more intelligible by the illustrative specimens presently to be given.

VOCABULARY OF THIS PERIOD.

42. Throughout this period the vocabulary remained *purely Saxon*, so far as the written language was concerned. Scarcely any Roman words are to be met with in the Saxon Chronicle. A curious instance, it has been observed, is the word '*peace*' instead of the A.S. 'friþ from freó=free. The peace that was the result of *freódom*, and suggestive of it, could, indeed, exist no longer for the disheartened and down-trodden native. The death-like calm that succeeded the ruthless Norman devastations was sufficiently well expressed, thought the simple Saxon chronicler, by one of their own weak, meaningless terms. Layamon's great work consists, according as it is arranged, of either about 14,000 long or 32,000 short verses, yet contains not quite *fifty* French words in the older text, as left by him. There is a more recent MS. of the poem, referred to the reign of Henry III., perhaps about 1250, in which *thirty* of these are retained, and upwards of *forty* others introduced, making altogether about *seventy*, which, at an average of eight words to each long line, gives a proportion of one to 1,600.

SPECIMENS—SAXON CHRONICLE.

43. In order to convey to the eye, and through it to the mind, an idea of the difference between A.S. and Broken Saxon, the two following illustrative specimens are proposed. In No. I., a piece of the S. Chr., we have endeavoured, with the help of Rask and Spalding's valuable notes, to restore to the pure standard, as it would have been written in the days of Alfred or of Ælfric. In No. II., by way of further illustration for the classical student, a literal Latin version of the same piece is given, *grammatically correct.* Then a presumed *Broken Latin* and Italian version, which will help to show how Latin gradually merged into the modern vernacular. Some idea may thus be formed of the manner in which synthetic languages generally tend to lose their grammatical inflexions, and so become analytic. The wonderful influence that a mere shifting back of the *accent* has in producing this result, by *necessarily weakening* strong case and verbal endings, is here put in a striking manner. Take the word *pervenérunt*, and transfer the accent one syllable back; it becomes difficult at once to pronounce the final *t*, and the word is probably pervénerun at first, and then (the *liquid n* being dropped, for want of support) pervénero, or, as now written, pervénnero. That this tendency to throw back the accent, with similar results, existed even in classic times, has been abundantly shown by Donaldson in *Varronianus*, omnibus modis = omnímodis = omnímode, amavérunt = amárunt, etc.

Specimens—Saxon Chronicle. 59

I.—SAXON CHRONICLE, A.D. 1137.

Written some time after Stephen's death, 1154, describing the miseries inflicted by the Norman nobles on the natives during his reign.*

(a) Ilí swencton þá wreccan menn þœs landes mid castel-
(b) Hí swencten the wrecce men of-þe-land mid castel-
(c) *They harassed the wretched men of the land with castle-*

(a) weorcum. Þa þá castelas wœron gemacod þá fyldon
(b) weorces. Tha the castles waren maked thá fylden
(c) *works. When the castles were made, then filled*

(a) hí (hí) mid yfelum mannum. Þa namon hí þá
(b) hi mid yuele men. Tha namen hi þá
(c) *they (them) with evil men. Then took they the*

(a) menn þá hí wéndon þæt ænig gód hœfdon bátwá
(b) men þe hí wenden thæt ani gód hefden báthe
(c) *men that they thought that any goods had, both*

(a) nihtes and dages. Man hengon up bý þám fótum,
(b) be nihtes and be dæies. Me henged up bi the fét,
(c) *by night and by day. Men (they) hanged up by the feet,*

(a) and smucon heom mid fúlum sméoce : man dyde gecnottede
(b) and smoked heom mid fúl smoke : me dide cnotted
(c) *and smoked them with foul smoke : man did knotted*

(a) strengas abútan heora heafod, and wriðe oð hit eode to
(b) strenges abúton here hæved, and wrythen to-that it gæde to
(c) *strings about their head, and twisted until it went to*

(a) þám brægenum.—(Bodl. Laud text, Thorpe's ed., p. 382.)
(b) the hærnes.
(c) *the brains.*

II.—THE SAME IN LATIN, BROKEN LATIN, AND ITALIAN.

(a) Ipsi afflixerunt illos miserandos homines illius terræ cum
(b) Issi afflíxeron illi miserandi homini de illa terra cum
(c) Essi afflissero quelli miserandi uomini della terra con

---

* (a) = Anglo-Saxon and Latin.   (b) = Broken Saxon and Broken Latin.   (c) = Modern English and Italian.

III.—*Broken Saxon Period.*

(*a*) castellis munitis.   Quando illa castella fuerunt facta,   tum
(*b*) castelli muniti.   Quando illi castelli fúeron facti, ad illa hora
(*c*) castelli muniti.   Quando quei castelli furono fatti,   allora

(*a*) impleverunt illa ipsi (cum) malis hominibus.   Tum
(*b*) impleveron illi issi cum mali homini.   Ad-la hora
(*c*) empiron . -li essi con mali uomini.   Allora

(*a*) prehenderunt ipsi illos homines quos ipsi existimaverunt qui
(*b*) prehénderon issi illi homini qui issi istimáveron qui
(*c*) presero essi quegli uomini che essi stimarono che

(*a*) aliqua bona haberent et noctu et die.   Suspenderunt
(*b*) aliqui boni haberen et de nocte et de die.   Suspenderon
(*c*) alcuni beni avessero e di notte e di dì.   Sospesero

(*a*) pedibus et fumigaverunt illos cum immundo fumo. Alii
(*b*) per pedes et fumigáveron illi cum immundo fumo. Alteri
(*c*) pei piedi ed affumicaron- li con immondo fumo. Altri

(*a*) fecerunt nodatas chordas circa illorum capita, et contorserunt
(*b*) féceron nodate chorde circa illoru capiti, et contorseron
(*c*) fecero nodate corde circa i loro capi, e contorsero

(*a*)   donec   illæ pervenerunt ad cerebrum.
(*b*) ad-finemquod ille perveneron ad   cerebro.
(*c*)   finchè   quelle pervennero al   cervello.

By way of further illustration, and to show that the Semi-Latin here assumed is not without precedent, a curious scrap is added of what Cantú calls 'i primordii della lingua Italiana.' It contains some directions of a chemist referred to the year 770, when the language was in a state of disorganization, but not to the same extent as is presumed in our specimen.

'Cuse ipsas pelles; laxa dissicare, batte lamina, et post illa battuta, per martellum adequatur, tam de latum quam de longum: scaldato illo in foco, batte et tene illud cum tanalea ferrea; sed tornatur de intro in foras: dextende eum; ibi scalda; pone ad battere; settecientur; modicum laxa stare; et lixa illud...imple carbonibus, et decoque... josu ligna, et sus carbones—et si una long fuerit vel curta, per martellum adequatur.'—' Schiarimenti e noti,' iv.

One great advantage of our early English remains is, that they enable us to trace the progress of the language, step by step, from the remotest times, and render such a work as the present possible, which, for want of a similar literature, the Italians and French could scarcely attempt successfully.

LAYAMON.

44. An extract from Layamon will help to show how very much the language had fallen off since the last specimen from the Sax. Chr. He tells us, in the beginning of his poem, that he was a priest of Ernley, on the Severn, and as he was a native of Worcestershire, it is supposed that he used the dialect of the West of England. It is, 'at any rate, clearly southern as opposed to northern, and western as opposed to eastern.'—Craik, 'Outlines.' Much has been written upon the *nunnation*, or redundant use of *n*, and other peculiarities of this dialect, such as the plural in *th*, *we loveth*, *u* for *i*, as *dude*=dide, etc. He 'seems to have halted between two languages, the written and the spoken. Now, he gives us what appears to be the old English dialect of the west; and, a few sentences farther, we find ourselves entangled in all the peculiarities of the A.S.'—'Engl. Rhythms,' II. In truth, not over much importance can be attached to his language, beyond what was stated above.* Neither it nor any of the literature of

---

* The peculiarities of Layamon's grammar may be briefly summed up as follows :—The endings *a*, *an*, and *on* weakened to *e* and *en*; gender disregarded ; neuter pl. nouns take mas. forms.; fem. adjectival and pronominal endings neglected ; definite and indefinite declensions confused ; preposition *to* extended to the infinitive ; many strong verbs become weak , final *e* frequently elided ; government of prepositions becomes uncertain ; plural in *es* becomes very general ; *of* used for the genitive in the later MS. (1250) ; frequent nunnation in the first MS. ; *shall* and *will* are used now for the first time as auxiliaries, in this

these times was much read or even generally known outside the monasteries where it was composed. It could not have exercised the slightest influence on that which followed, for it never could be considered a correct standard worthy to be imitated by subsequent writers. Literature it was not at all, in the strict sense of the word, as we take it to be, that is, truth expressed in *beautiful and elegant* language. Such could not exist at a time when the means of creating the latter of these ingredients were wanting. This specimen from the account of the Battle of Bath, has been also put into A.S. like the foregoing.

LAYAMON, A.D. 1200.

(a) Þær wæron Sæxisce menn: folca ealra ærmeste;
(b) Ther weoren Sæxisce men: folken alre ærmest;
(c) *There were Saxon men: of folk all wretchedest;*

(a) And þa Alemainiscan menn: geomerestan ealra leoda:
(b) And thá Alemainisce men: geomerest alre leoden:
(c) *And the Alemannish men: saddest of all people:*

(a) Arthur mid his sweorde: fæge-scipe worhte:
(b) Arthur mid his sweorde: fœic-scipe wurhte:
(c) *Arthur with his sword: death-work wrought:*

(a) Eall þæt he smát (tó): hit wæs sona forgedón:
(b) Al that he smat to: hit wes sone fordon:
(c) *All that he smote to: it was soon done-for:*

(a) Eall wæs se cyning abolgen: swá byð se wilda bár—
(b) Al wæs the king abolgen: swá bith the wilde bar—
(c) *All was the king enraged: as is the wild boar.*

A RHYMING POEM.

45. The following is given as almost the only extant specimen of a Saxon rhyming poem, and as otherwise interesting. It belongs to the Norman period, and occurs

showing 'closer uniformity to the present practice than is found in many works of even as late a date as the 14th century.'—*Marsh, English Language*, 1862.

at p. 222 of vol. I. of Hickes' 'Linguarum Veterum Septentrionalium Thesaurus.' A translation and notes are added, in further illustration of the state of the language about this time.

He wot hwet ðencheð,[1] und hwet doð[1]	He wots what think and what do
Alle quike wihte.[2]	All living beings.
Nis[3] no Louerd swich is Christ,	No lord is such as Christ,
Ne no King swich is Drihte.[4]	Nor King such as is the Lord
Hevene and erþe and all þat is,	Heaven and earth and all that is,
Biloken[5] is on his honde.	Locked up is in his hand.
He deð all þæt his wille is,	He doth all that his will is,
On sea and ec[6] on londe.	On sea and eke on land.
He witeð and wealdeð alle þing,	He knows and wieldeth all things,
He iscop[7] alle sceafte,	He made all creatures,
He whrote fis on þer[8] sea	He wrought fish in the sea
And forgeles[9] on þar[8] lefte.	And fowls in the air.
He is ord[10] abuten orde,	He is beginning without beginning,
And ende abuten ende ;	And end without end ;
He one is eure on eche[11] stede,[12]	He is ever one in every place,
Wende[13] wer þu wende.	Wend where thou wend.

1. Thinketh and doeth, pl., not singular, ð being the proper ending of the pl. pres. indic. as shown in § 23. Observe the trace of Norman influence on the orthography in the spelling of ðencheð, where *ch* is used for *k* or *c*.

2. Alle quike wihte in correct A.S. would be : ealle cwice wihta = all quick wights. Quick still survives in the Biblical expression 'the quick and the dead ;' and Spenser uses *wight* always in the same sense as here. Thus :—

    Some blisfull houres at last must needes appeare,
    Else should afflicted wights oft-times despeire.
                          Faerie Queen, V. iii. 1.

3. Nis = ne is = is not, followed by another negative, two or even more negatives in Saxon and Early English being used to strengthen the negation. Thus Chaucer :—

    He nevir yit no vilonye ne sayde
    In al his lyf unto no maner wight.
                       Prologue to Cant. Tales.

4. Drihten, a common word for Lord in A.S. It seems to have unaccountably disappeared from the language towards the close of the present period.

III.—*Broken Saxon Period.*

This is from the Digby MS. of a poem, known as 'The Moral Ode,' of which several versions are extant. An earlier text from the famous Lambeth MS. 487 has been published by Dr. Morris in his 'Old English Homilies,' first series, pp. 158-183, and another from the Trinity Col. MS., in the second series, pp. 220-232. The Lambeth text, which Dr. Morris believes to be the oldest (before 1200), is here added for the purpose of comparison with the foregoing. In the Preface to first series he describes it as 'an excellent sermon in verse,' and it certainly is a very fine poem, which deserves to be more generally known:—

> ' He wat wet þenkeð and hwet doð alle quike wihte.
> Nis na lauerd swich se is Crist. ne king swuch ure drihten.
> Houene and orðe and al þet is biloken is in his honde.
> He deð al þet his wil is a wettre and alonde.
> He makede fisses in þe se and fuzeles in þe lifte.
> He wit and waldeð alle þing and scop alle seefte.
> He is hord buten horde and ende buten ende.
> He ane is eure an ilche stude wende þer þu wende.'—ll. 79-86.

---

5. Biloken = belocen, past part. of belucan = to lock up. This is an instance of a strong verb having become weak in modern English.

6. ec = eac = eke = the German auch.

7. iscop for gescop, from gesceapan = to shape = to make, to create. This verb has also become weak, besides losing its higher meaning. Compare the German schaffen, schuff, geschaffen, and *scop* = the shaper = the maker = the poet (ποιέω) in the Beowulf.

8. on þer = in the, þer = dat. fem. of the definite article, as in § 17. Compare the German : in der See.

9. forgeles, evidently for fogeles = fugelas, from fugel = fowl. Note the pl. ending *as* weakened to *es*.

10. ord = the German *ur*, as in Ur-sprung, and the Latin *or*, as in origo.

11. eche = æle, for ælcere, dat. fem. agreeing with

12. Stede = stead = place, as in the expression instead of = the French au lieu de. Compare also the German stadt.

13. Wende is a word of two syllables, final *e* being always pronounced in pure A.S. and mostly in Broken Saxon and Early English.

QUESTIONS.

32. What is the Transition Period? Its greatest extent? Subdivisions? Nature of these? Proper date of the Broken Saxon?

33. When did good A.S. cease to be *written*? Craik thinks it may have ceased to be *spoken* long before this.

34. The corruption of the language is differently accounted for. State the three views (*a*), (*b*), (*c*).

35. Explain accurately the nature of a *synthetic* as opposed to an *analytic* language. Which seems the most ancient state? Show that speech runs quite as readily from a *simple* to a *composite* state, as the other way. English appears to prove this?

36. There is *intrinsic* evidence of decay in A.S., which proves that it must have broken up independently of the Norman Conquest?

37. Still this event exercised a negative and indirect action on this tendency, therefore view (*a*) is erroneous, (*b*) partly true, (*c*) correct?

38. Mr. Guest's theory seems to be *the very reverse* of truth?

39. What is the general nature of the *grammar* during this stage? What changes occurred in the verb?

40. In the noun a preference is shown for one declension? Jacob Grimm, in attributing this to an indirect action of the French tongue, exhibits a greater knowledge of A.S. and modern English than of the intermediate stages of the language?

41. Change in the adjective? Gender? Article? Pronoun? Syntax?

42. What amount of Norman words were adopted into the *written* language during this period? One remarkable instance?

43. Show from the illustrative specimens the powerful influence a mere shifting of the *accent* seems to exercise generally on all composite languages. Explain its nature and cause.

44. Who was Layamon? In what dialect is he supposed to have written? None of the writings of this period could have had much influence on the subsequent *written*, much less *spoken* language?

SECTION IV.

EARLY ENGLISH PERIOD (1200–1350).

EARLY ENGLISH PERIOD ONE OF RECONSTRUCTION—GRAMMAR—VOCABULARY—THE ORMULUM—PRONUNCIATION—SPECIMENS.

NATURE AND EXTENT OF THE EARLY ENGLISH PERIOD.

46. We are still in the Transition Period of the language, and must continue in it until we arrive at something fixed or settled, so far as any living speech can attain to such a state. But there is a marked difference between the present stage and the last, similar to that which exists between the operation of taking down an old tottering edifice, and that of renewing it. Broken Saxon corresponds to the process of breaking up, this period and the next to that of rebuilding. These have, therefore, been called respectively periods of *dissolution* and of *reconstruction*. Until the one was effected, the other could not begin. This took place, we have seen, about the year 1200. Here, then, will begin a new era, and here we are to look for the first dawnings of a language to which the name of *English*, in the modern sense, may be applied. The whole of the *reconstruction* stage has been called *Old* English, and must evidently last until the language is completely formed. But, for the better understanding of the subject, it has been commonly subdivided into two other periods, the 'Early English' and 'Middle English.' To the first of these we have assigned the same number of years as to the Broken

Saxon, 150, from 1200 to 1350. This, we shall see, is not arbitrary, but marks a distinct change, which set in about the latter date.

FUSION OF SAXON AND NORMAN ELEMENTS.

47. It is not a little curious that the proper history of the English *people*, as opposed to that of the *country*, dates from the same year, 1200, or thereabouts. 'Here commences,' says Macaulay, 'the history of the English nation.' For it was now that began to take place the fusion of race, language, and institutions, which resulted in the nationality as it is still constituted. Hitherto there were two distinct and hostile peoples in the land, each speaking its own language. But now the two races, and the two languages, though not to the same extent, were blended together in the proportion that still obtains. The almost total separation of England from the mainland, which took place on the loss of Normandy, about this time, was chiefly instrumental in bringing about and consolidating the union. With respect to the language, the change for the present was rather one of *extension* than of *absorption*. Its sphere of action was enlarged when it came to be recognised by all parties, Anglo-Norman as well as Anglo-Saxon, as the sole and exclusive national speech. But 'the happy marriage,' as it has been called, 'in our tongue, of the languages of the north and south,' was not accomplished till the next period. It could be brought about only by a sort of compromise, so to say, between the two rivals. Some mutual sacrifice was required at the hands of both parties, for which neither was yet quite prepared. Thus, at length, it happened that the old inhabitants, while retaining the primitive speech, yet admitted into it a considerable foreign element; and, again, the Anglo-Normans, in laying aside the French language, preserved a great portion of its idioms and words, mixing them freely with their newly adopted speech. In this way is explained the fact, not to be lost sight of, that not until the next period was Saxon to any extent affected by Normanisms, and that without such a union of the two races it never would have been so affected. One or other of the two speeches would have gained the upper hand, and remained the undisputed possessor of the country, and the language at the present day would be either *pure* Norman or *pure* Saxon, or very nearly so.

CHANGE OF ALPHABET—ORTHOGRAPHY.

48. A change occurred about this time, which seems to point out a decided step towards modern English. As long as the language remained Saxon, whether pure or broken, the old alphabet was generally retained; but this seems to have been gradually laid aside for the Norman, after the last efforts were made to keep up that system. Warton, in his 'History of English Poetry,' observes that Mabillon 'was mistaken in asserting that the Saxon way of writing was entirely abolished in England at the time of the Norman Conquest. . . . An intermixture of the Saxon character is common in English and Latin MSS. before the reign of Edward III., but of a few types only.' This adoption of an alphabet, not perfectly corresponding to the old, helped to increase the state of confusion in which the orthography then was, and remained for centuries after. 'Not only are almost all the words spelled differently by different authors, but even by the same author, in the same book, in the same page, and frequently in the same line.'—'Diversions of Purley.' At a period of reconstruction, of course, no standard can exist to be followed implicitly by all, and each writer being left to decide for himself, the result must be confusion and utter absence of anything like uniformity. So uncertain is the orthography, that no importance can be attached to the manner of spelling any word during this period, except so far as it may help to indicate the current pronunciation, as we shall see was the case with the Ormulum.

VARIOUS LANGUAGES EMPLOYED IN LITERATURE.

49. What is true of the orthography is equally true of the *grammar* throughout the whole of this stage of the language. It varies considerably with writers supposed to be contemporary, nor is any author always consistent with himself. Consequently grammar, as the art of teaching the proper use of words, cannot be said to have existed at all. But the efforts that were made at composition had this advantage, that they helped gradually to mould the language into something fixed and satisfactory. Our opportunities of examining its structure at this epoch are not over numerous. The times generally were not favourable to letters, and the few men who did devote themselves to literature were divided between the claims of no less than three rival languages. *Saxon* was employed in the national ballad poetry, a species of literature which is the earliest in almost every country. It had, probably, existed during the Broken Saxon times, but now rose into importance in proportion as the language became universally spoken by all classes. *French* continued still to be employed almost exclusively at the court, and in the composition of romances, or what would now be called the fashionable literature of the day. The monks wrote all their learned works in *Latin*, besides some considerable productions in their native tongue. Indeed the constant employment of Latin all along by this class of writers must be looked upon as a most fortunate circumstance. It, probably, saved the English language, or at least prevented it from sinking into the condition of a mere *patois*, such as the Flemish has continued to be owing to the general use of *French* by the Belgians in *Literature*. In England, the literary world being divided between three rivals, the native speech, having numbers on its side, ultimately succeeded in gaining the ascendant. The case might have been otherwise, had all parties united their energies in endeavouring to render Norman literature *national* in the island. The first great genius that arose, say Chaucer, finding the Saxon totally unfit for literary purposes, the necessary result of the neglect of 300 years, would have been compelled to use the French tongue, if he hoped to hand down his name to posterity. Without pursuing the argument further, it must be allowed that, whatever influence all the literature of the Broken Saxon and Early English Periods (1066–1350) has had, both positively and negatively, in moulding the language into its present shape, is largely due to a body of men whose services are too often apt to be lost sight of.

DIFFERENCE BETWEEN BROKEN SAXON AND EARLY ENGLISH.

50. In general it may be said that the *grammar* of the popular ballad poetry is more advanced than that of the rhyming chronicles, and of the Ormulum. The latter works seem to have been formed more upon the *literary* language of the preceding age, whilst the former may have developed itself at once, and independently, out of the spoken tongue, which, it has been shown, was, from the remotest times, always more English in the modern sense than the written. At the same time, it should be observed, that the present copies of most of the old songs are considerably modernised, even as they are printed in Percy's 'Reliques.' The 'Battle of Otterburne' cannot, in its actual form, be placed further back than the year 1450. though referring to an event which occurred in the year 1388. In general, no sort of reliance can be placed upon the dates to which the greater portion of old English poetry has been assigned, least of all to Warton's chronological arrangement. In his History of English Poetry he alludes to a translation of the O. and

N. T. in verse, which he believes 'to have been made before the year 1200.' This would make it Broken Saxon, but it will be seen, by comparing the following passage with the specimens in the last section, that it is quite English, and intelligible even in its old orthography:—

> '*Oure* ladi and *hire* sistur stoden under the Roode,
> And Seint John and Marie.Magdaleyne with wel sori moode :
> *Ur* ladi biheold hire swete son i-brought in gret peyne,
> *Ffor* mounes gultes nouthen *her* and nothing *for* myne.
> Marie *weop* wel sore and bitter teres leet,
> The teres fullen uppon the ston doun at hire feet.'

The different forms, *hire* and *her*, *oure* and *ur*, *ffor* and *for*, will serve to illustrate what has just been said of the irregular orthography of these times. *Weop=wept* is an instance of a *strong* conjugation now obsolete, but retained in Old English. See its gradual changes in the comparative table, Section VI. § 86, and compare it with *weoxon* in this section, § 53. The main difference of structure, between this period and the Broken Saxon, consists in a further softening and weakening without a total rejection of certain grammatical inflexions, the result of which was to render them *less important* in construing, and to bring into play an increased number of *relational* words to perform the functions, and often to supply the place, of the enfeebled case and verbal endings. This gives such a new air to the language that, in virtue of it, we are now justified in calling it English. A practical test of the effects of this change may be had by endeavouring to turn a piece of Broken Saxon and of Old into Modern English. It will be found, as a rule, that the latter will be intelligible with the aid of a glossary and occasional notes, whilst the former will require an interlinear translation, with a certain amount of grammatical analysis. For instance, the following passage from Layamon is sufficiently intelligible in the appended Old English version, while all the words of the text in Italics still require further explanation :—

'Wace wæs ihoten
He wol couðe writen
And he *hoe* yef *thare*
Adhelen Alienor,
The waes Henries quene
The *heyes Kinges.*'

'Wace was i-het (hight)
He wel cude writé
And he it gav to the
Noble Elleanor
That was Henres quene
The heye (strong) Kingé.'

GRAMMAR—FINAL *e* SYLLABIC.

51. The inflexional forms were most commonly weakened by substituting in final syllables, -*e* for the Saxon -*a*, -*e*, -*u*, -*o*, -*na*, *ra*, *um*, etc., distinguishing the noun and verb endings. 'In the old English, all these were represented by the final -*e*, and the loss of the final -*e* is characteristic of our modern dialect. It is obvious that either of these changes must have brought about a new language. The confusion of the vowels, or the loss of the final -*e*, was the confounding of tense and person, of case and number — in short, of those grammatical forms to which language owes its precision and its clearness. Other forms were to be sought for before our tongue could again serve the purposes of science or of literature.'—'English Rhythms,' II. The forms, or rather expedients, here alluded to, were the particles or relational words, as already stated. The plural of *eall=all*, and the present indicative of *bringan=bring*, would be thus inflected in the three stages of the language hitherto investigated :—

Anglo-Saxon.	*Broken Saxon.*	*Early English.*
N. A. ealle,	ealé,	alle.
D. Abl. eallum,	tó ealé,	to allé.
Gen. ealra,	alré,	of allé.
ic bringe,	bringe,	bringe.
þu bringst,	bringast,	bringest.
he bringð,	bringedh,	bringeth.
pl. bringað,	bringadh,	bringeth (see Sec V. § 67).

Here it should be observed that this final -*e* was in Early English, perhaps *never mute*, and in Middle English generally constituted a syllable when it represented the inflexions of the old language. The importance of this, in the scansion of our early poets, is obvious, and will be again referred to in the next section.

INFINITIVE—GERUND—PRESENT PARTICIPLE

52. Other changes that occur are not so uniform. Some of them come earlier, some a little later on; some are met with in one writer and not in another of the same time, nor even with any regularity in the same work. There are symptoms already manifesting themselves of a desire to shake off the final *n* of the infinitive, and all distinction now ceases to be observed between this mood and the gerund in -*enne*, -*anne*. In A.S., the particle *tó* was *never* used with the inf., *always* with the gerund. The confusion of the two was occasioned by not observing this rule. It gave rise to the modern inf., which, in reality, is a sort of verbal noun, governed by a preposition, as the A.S. gerund was said to be the dative case of the inf., with its proper case ending : *witan*=scire, tó *witanne*=ad sciendum, both represented by the modern *to know*; so : *swerian, to swerigenne = to swear, writan, to writanne=to write,* etc. Connected with this was the gradual change of the active participle from -*ende* to -*and*, -*inge* and -*ing: swerigénde = sweriging=swearing, writende = writinge=writing, beonde= beánd=being, hæbbende=hebbend = haband= having.* The following scraps are of the same age, about 1300 or earlier; yet one retains the old form, while the other has already adopted the new :—

Witness of lourd is ever trewe
Wisdom *servand* to littell newe :
Lourd's rihtwisnesse riht hertes famand,
But of lourd is liht eghen *sighand*, etc.

Almightin louerd, hegest **kinge**,
Thu give me seli *timinge*
To thau men this werdes *bigin-- inge*.
The lauerd God to *wurthinge*, etc.

IV.—Early English Period.

The change arose from confounding the A.S. *-ung* and *-ing*, common in *verbal* nouns, with the active participle of the verb, the meaning being often much alike, from *grétan* (to greet) *grétende=greeting;* but *gréting*=a greeting (verbal noun); from *halgian* (to hallow), act. part.=*halgigende*= *hallowing*, and verbal noun *halgung=a hallowing*, or consecration; so *clænsung=a cleansing*, *hwistlung*=a whistling, *byrging*=a tasting. This is the reason why our active participles so readily become nouns: the *rising* sun, early *rising*. They are often, in fact, quite as much *nouns* as participles, which is the case wherever *-ing* has a corresponding A.S. verbal noun in *-ung* or *-ing;* such are not participles turned into substantives, as grammars parse them, but real verbal nouns, which have displaced the proper active participles in *-ende*, wherever they are used as such. Both endings coexisted side by side from the earliest times, and continued to do so in the Scottish dialect down to the sixteenth century, without the distinction being always observed. Barbour has both lik*and* and lik*ing* used correctly in the following passage from his 'Bruce:'—

> Such thyngis that are lik*and* (part.)
> Tyll mannys hear*ing* ar pleas*and* . . .
> Hors or hund or othir thing
> That war ples*and* to thar lik*ing* (noun).

So a prose writer in 1572 has 'in the print-*ing*' and 'discord in teach-*ing*' as verbal nouns, but say-*and*, kenn-*and*, as participles; *and* is exceedingly rare in Chaucer, the substitution having been fairly established in the southern dialect during the present period. We may now, perhaps, understand such idioms as *a-fishing*, *a-hunting*, *a-sleep*= *a-sleeping*. *a-wake*=*a-waking*, where *a* was in A.S. and Early E. the preposition *on = in:* 'with that he fell *on slepe*.'—Holinshed. So *on lyve=alive*, in which expressions *on* evidently governs not a participle, but a *noun*, in the ordinary way: 'The Erle of Salisburye was taken *on lyfe*=

in his lifetime=alive: aboard=on board, and on side=on one side=aside in the phrase, 'for hope of life was set on side.'— Hall.

COMPARATIVE TABLE OF EARLY ENGLISH FORMS.

53. The following table, containing some of the forms most used during the three stages hitherto examined, may help to convey a comprehensive idea of the gradual transition, and of the changes that occurred during the present period.

		Anglo-Saxon.	Broken Saxon.	Early English.	Modern.
Pronoun.	{	heom	to heom	to hom	to them
		heora	here	of hire	of their
		þære	to thære	to thare	to the
		seó	heó	ho, scho	she
Noun.	{	suna	sunes	of the suné	of the son
		dóhtra	dóhtras	dauhtren*	daughters
		sweostrum	to the swestres	to the swistren*	to the sisters
Adjective.	{	se góda	the godé	the godé	the good
		smœlra	smalre	of smalles	of small (pl.)
		strengre	strangor	stranger	stronger
		strengste	strengeste	strangest	strongest
Verb.	{	wœron	weoren	weren	were
		hœfdon	hafden	heddén	had (pl.)
		hengon	hengen	hengeth	hanged (pl.)
		sagde	sæde	seide	said
		hi singað	hi singedh	hi singth	they sing
		beón	byn	bón	may be
		wyrcan	wircen	wirchén	to work
		axian	axien	axen	to ask
Participle.	{	geboren	gebore	iboré	born
		gelufod	gelufed	ylovéd	loved
		to lufigenne } lufian	to lufian	to loven	to love
		lufigende	lufigend	lovand	loving
		bœrnende	bernend	byrninge	burning
		weoxon	woxen	wexide	waxed pl. (grew)
Adverb, etc.	{	hwænne	hwane	wane	when
		feor	fear	for	far
		bútan	búten	buté	but, etc.

VOCABULARY—NORMAN ELEMENT.

54. While the structure of the language is thus rapidly becoming English, the vocabulary remains still almost purely Saxon. The amount of Norman that was now

* For certain plurals in *en*, occurring in Old E. and not found in A.S., see Sec. VI., § 87.

introduced it is impossible to determine; for it varies according to the fancy or inclination of the writer. The Ormulum is nearly as free of Gallicisms as the language of Layamon, while in other writers, especially Robert of Gloucester, French words seem to be introduced with a certain facility, implying that they must have been current in the language at the time: this *noble* sone—in this *manere*. Bute he come to *amendement*—to ys *contrei* drow, etc. Perhaps this is what Robert de Brunne complains of when he says that many of the compositions of these times were become quite unintelligible to a common audience; for the great body of Normanisms now incorporated in the language, passed into it through the current literature of these times, and were, when first used, what we should call learned and pedantic terms, of course not generally understood by the Saxon-speaking and illiterate portions of the population:—

> Thai sayd in so quaynte Inlis
> That mony one wate not what it is,
> And forsooth I couth nought
> So strange Inglis as thai wrought.

In the next section it will be seen that the great influx of French words did not take place until the Anglo-Normans began to cultivate English and to substitute it for French in literature.

There were, nevertheless, certain classes of French words which, it will be safe to say, had found their way into the *spoken* language by this time, though we may not be able to fix the precise date of their introduction. A reference to the social condition of the two races will help to discover their nature. The Anglo-Norman lords of the land, to protect themselves against the Saxon rebel, began, soon after the invasion, to build strongholds all over the island, and to people them with their foreign retainers. Each of these fastnesses thus became, so to say, a little French colony, speaking the French language and holding little converse with the Saxon tillers of the soil. Here justice was administered and all legal questions settled by foreign lawyers in a foreign tongue. In the same way all pleadings were conducted in French at the King's court, so that in every instance the natives were compelled, for the sake of their suits, to plead in that tongue, or, at least, to acquaint themselves with its legal technicalities. The great body of such words are therefore Norman: *plaintiff, defendant, jury, judge, justice, magistrate, chancellor, attorney, court, fine, damages, parliament, legist, tax, assess, mulct, o-yes* (*oyez* = hear ye), *oyer and terminer* (to hear and determine).

The Norman barons and knights were at this time the most chivalrous and warlike in Europe. Hence the language of war and chivalry is almost exclusively French: *gallant, champion, courtesy, challenge, tournament, soldier, militia, arms, to march, battle,* etc.

All the higher dignities of the Church were filled with Normans or Italians. They occasioned a second accession of church words, such as: *sacrament, friar, altar, sacrifice, ceremony, religion, tonsure, sermon, prayer, devotion, piety, idolatry, pagan, scandal, interdict.*

The passion of the Norman kings and nobles for the *chase* enriched the language with many French terms relating to this subject, without, however, in this instance superseding the old stock supplied by their Saxon predecessors. Hence we have side by side: the *hunt* and the *chase, hawk* and *falcon, fox* and *renard, rabbit* and *coney, hare* and *leveret, course, race* and *race-course, brace* and *couple, wood* and *forest, thicket* and *copse* (*couper*), *underwood* and *copsewood,* etc.

The rude native had been hitherto content to eat his *ox* and *cow,* his *calf, sheep,* and *swine,* or *hog,* as he does to this day his *lamb* and *kid;* but in course of time he learned from his Norman rulers that these animals were only fit for human food under the softened name of *beef, veal, mutton, pork.* To such an extent is the language of cookery French that one would almost suppose the art was unknown previous to the Conquest. Thus it is that words have a peculiar significance of their own. They often speak eloquently of a people's glory and reverses, of prosperity and disaster, of freedom and bondage, of generations of tyranny sullenly resisted, sometimes hopelessly, sometimes with a happy issue.

The same story of Norman tyranny and Saxon thraldom is told by a certain class of native terms, which, without being altogether set aside, have yet been displaced from their proper position by corresponding French words. 'We may trace, I think, a permanent record of this depression in the fact that a vast number of Teutonic words, which have a noble sense in the kindred language of Germany, and evidently had once such in the A.S., have forfeited this in whole or in part, have been contented to take a lower place, while, in most instances, a word of the Latin moiety of the language has assumed the place which they have vacated.' —'English, Past and Present.' Thus *tapfer* is *courageous* in German, but *dapper* in English is only *spruce* or *smart*. Some of the instances, however, here cited by Dr. Trench, are rather examples of the danger of building theories on words before they are thoroughly sifted. *Haut* may have been *skin* in German, but *hýd=hide*, never meant in A.S. any thing more dignified than it now does; *hýd-gild* was 'money paid to escape flogging.' If there is no idea of *too great haste* attached to the German word *rasch*, there certainly always was to the English *rash*, from A.S. *hreosan*=to rush violently. So the primary sense of *beam* in A.S. was a *beam*, *post*, *stock*, and even *splint*, though the German *baum* may imply a 'living tree,' as opposed to 'dead timber.' In these words, therefore, there is no trace of French action on the Saxon portion of the vocabulary.

ROMANCE AND LATIN ELEMENT.

55. As French is itself an offshoot of Latin, the class of words introduced during the present stage has been called

'Latin of the Third Period,' or *Norman Latin*, as distinguished from the *Roman* and *Church* Latin of the Saxon times. As Latin is, again, a member of the great Indo-European Family, it naturally possesses a number of radical words common also to the A.S. Hence the difficulty that sometimes arises of determining the true origin of such English words as correspond in these two languages. We must, in such cases, be guided by the *nature* of the words themselves. If they are concerned with the business of every-day life, or expressive of notions not above the comprehension of the most illiterate during the previous stage, the presumption will be that they came directly from the A.S., otherwise the chances will be in favour of a Romance origin. The following are a few words which, *etymologically*, might be equally well derived from the A.S. or Romance:—

Romance.	Anglo-Saxon.	English.	Romance.	Anglo-Saxon.	English.
me,	me,	me.	mulgere,	meolcian,	to milk.
te,	the,	thee.	jugum,	geoc,	joke.
tu,	thu,	thou.	ives (if),	iw,	yew.
via,	weg,	way.	jardin,	gyrdan,	garden.
vermis,	wyrm,	worm.	gagner,	gewinnan,	win.
ventum,	wind,	wind.	loi,	lag-lah,	law.
temps,	tima,	time.	long,	long,	long.
vinum,	win,	wine.	velle,	willan,	will.
jeune,	geong,	young.	vulg-us,	folc,	folk.
nord,	norð,	north.	insula,	ealand,	island.*
sud,	suð,	south.	guise,	wise,	wise.
ouest,	east,	east.	guerre,	wær,	war.
est,	west,	west.	dies,	dæg,	day.
nom,	nama,	name.	garder,	ward,	guard.
hesternus,	gystrandæg,	yester(day).	garantir,	warian,	warrant.
habere,	habban,	to have.	mens,	gemynd,	mind.

Romance† is here used in an extended sense to include

---

* *s* here is a later intrusion by wrongly assumed derivation from *insula*. It is always *iland* from *ealand*, down to the seventeenth century. The mistake arose from its apparent relation to *isle* = *île* = *insula*, and from the great source of such anomalies, ignorance of A.S.

† It should be observed, however, that many of these Romance terms, such as est, sud, jardin, guise, guerre, garder, &c., are themselves of Teutonic origin. French philologists estimate their number at about a thousand altogether, and they are generally such words as the Franks might be expected to retain, while gradually laying aside their own

both the Latin and French. It properly means such languages as are derived from the Latin or *Roman* tongue—

> ' Frankis spech is cald *romance*,
> So sais clerkes and men of France '—
> Robert de Brunne.

But the single reflection that all these terms must have been constantly in the mouths of the masses from pre-historic times will decide the question in favour of the A.S., though some of them may actually approach nearer to the Latin in form. For a parallel reason the following might seem to be either doubtful or Norman :—

Romance.	Anglo-Saxon.	English.	Romance.	Anglo-Saxon.	English.
tabula,	tæfl,	table.	vastare,	westan,	to *waste*.
vallum,	weal,	*wall*.	fluere,	fleuwan,	to *flow*.
guille,	wile,	*wile*, guile.	figere,	fegan,	to fix.
miscere,	miscan,	to *mix*.	curare,	carian,	to *care*.
mons,	munt,	mount.	spolium,	spillan,	spoil.
sugere,	sucan,	*suck*.	habilis,	abal,	able.
choisir,	ceosan,	*choose*.			

Here the words in *Italics* are now properly referred to the A.S. *Choose* must be Saxon, because it belongs to the *strong* conjugation : *choose, chose,* and *chase* (old), *chosen*. It is a rule that all foreign words are inflected according to weak forms. No French noun ever took the plur. in *-en*, no verb any other past tense and part. but *-ed*. We say legal--*ity*, but lawful-*ness*.

Formerly all the words in the two foregoing lists, and half the language besides, were derived from Latin, Greek, Hebrew, or anything but A.S.* Attention to these prin-

language and adopting the corrupt Latin spoken in Gaul when they settled there. A complete list of them may be seen in the Introduction to Brachet's *Dictionnaire Etymologique de la Langue Française*, Paris, Hetzel & Cie. In his *Historical Outlines*, pp. 256-9, Morris gives a list of such of them as have crept into English. But amongst them he includes arquebuss, bivouac, and some others of very recent date, and others again, such as champion, flatter, which are very doubtful.

* Minschew derives the inf. particle *to* from the Greek τὸ : to make = τὸ ποιεῖν. Others from the Latin *ad.*, and Sharp from the Hebrew.

ciples, and generally to the *nature* of the words we are comparing, is a great check upon the tendency, strongly developed in some minds, to push etymological investigations too far, and may help to prevent such fanciful derivations as *dream* from *drama*, 'because life is a drama, and drama is a dream' (Johnson's Preface); or *Constantinople* from *Constantine the Noble* (actually given by one writer); or *quaff* from *go off, quoff, quaff*, seriously proposed by Skinner; or *King Pepin* from ὅσπερ cited by H. Tooke: ὅσπερ—ἥπερ—ὅπερ—Diaper—Napkin—Nipkin—Pepkin—Pippin-King—King Pepin; or all the proper names of Genesis, from corresponding words or idioms in Flemish or Welsh, according to the humour of the writer.

THE ORMULUM—ITS DATE.

56. Of the literary remains of this period, the most interesting in the history of the language is the *Ormulum*, so called by the author from his own name,* *Orm* or *Ormin*. It consists of a metrical paraphrase of such portions of Scripture as are introduced into the service and offices of the Church, extending to about 10,000 long, or 20,000 short lines, as first edited by Dr. M. White of Oxford in 1852. In it all the peculiar features of the Old English dialect are strongly developed, and it is 'the oldest, the purest, and by far the most valuable specimen' of this stage of the language 'that time has left us' ('English Rhythms,' I.) Much diversity of opinion prevails as to the time of its composition. The work just cited assigns it to the twelfth century, and others even to the eleventh; but, to judge from intrinsic evidence, it cannot be placed much earlier than the middle of the thirteenth, if so early. It was, probably, written sometime between 1220 and 1250, or rather less than half a century after Layamon's

---

* þis boc iss nemmed Ormulum
Forrþi þatt Orm itt wrohhte.

'Brut.' Indeed its style, as compared with this production, exhibits the language in so very advanced a state, that we should be disposed, at first sight, to bring it forward still further, did we not remember that a few years in the infancy or in the old age of a language, produce greater changes than are apparent in many centuries of its maturity. We would almost venture to say, that the difference between the language of our time and that of the Ormulum, after a lapse of over 600 years, is considerably less than what is observable between it and that of the preceding age.

ITS ORTHOGRAPHY—PRONUNCIATION.

57. The orthography of the Ormulum is remarkable, as affording additional proof of the absence of any fixed standard for spelling at the time of its composition. Its author feeling that the great uncertainty of the orthography rendered it quite useless as a guide to the real pronunciation of words, and considering that this should be one of the first objects of a written tongue, proceeds to draw out a plan of his own, by which he hopes to attain to this result, and to which he accordingly attaches great importance, insisting upon a strict adherence to it on the part of all future copyists of his work.* Its chief characteristic consists in *always doubling the consonant following short vowels*, so as to make them *short* by position, just as they would be

* 'And whase wilenn shall þiss boc efft oþerr siþe writenn
   Hinn bidde ic þatt het write rihht swa summ þiss boc him tæcneþþ.
   All þwerrt ut affter þatt itt iss uppo þiss firrste bisne,
   Wiþþe all swike rime alls her iss sett wiþþ all se fele wordess ;
   And tatt he loke wel þatt he an bokstaff write twiyyes,
   Eggwhær þær itt uppo þiss boc iss writen o þatt wise.'

That is to say : And whoso shall will to write again another time, I bid him that he write it rightly, so as this book teacheth him entirely as it is upon this first pattern with all such measures as here are set, with just as many words, and that he look well that he write a letter twice where it upon this book is written in that wise.

Orthographic Systems.

said to be *long by position* in Latin or Greek prosody: sĕtt= set, thĭss=this, thătt=that, bĕttre=better, Gŏdd=God, but gōd=good; where it appears that vowels followed by *single* consonants are meant by him to be pronounced *long*. Great light is in this way thrown upon the current pronunciation at the time. 'If it was his rule always to leave the consonant single after the long or *name* sound (as in *mate, meet, mite, mote, mute*), and to double it after every vowel otherwise sounded, then .... we should learn that while *God, thus, till, up, will, his, off, wit, for, edge, back, it, with, on, that*, were all pronounced in his day as at present, with the *shut* sound, *thine, sheep, smite, child*, took as they now do, the *name* (long) sound; that the *e* in *legg* (*lay*) and in the first syllable of *seggde* (*said*), was sounded as in our *egg* . . . that *bun* was probably pronounced *boon, don, doon*,' etc. (Craik's 'Outlines,' 72.) This method does not appear to have survived its originator, for in the next period we find it superseded, at least by writers of the Anglo-Norman school, who introduced the *e* mute to lengthen the preceding vowel, leaving the consonant single when they wished it to be short: *sāle, sĕl; tāle, tĕl*, also *tell*. The appended comparative table of orthographic systems at different times employed may serve to throw some light on a matter sufficiently obscure, and which has not been hitherto fully explained:—

Anglo-Saxon.	Early English.	Middle English.	Modern.
\multicolumn{4}{c}{SHORT VOWELS.}			
can,	cann,	can,	can.
stif,	stiff,	stiff,	stiff.
God,	Godd,	God,	God.
	LONG VOWELS.		
gód,	god,	gode,	good.
œn,	on,	on,	one.
áð,	ath,	othe,	oath.
bár,	bor,	bore,	boar.
bán,	bon,	bone,	bone.
stœn,	ston,	stone,	stone.

IV.—*Early English Period.*

Anglo-Saxon.	Early English.	Middle English.	Modern.
LONG VOWELS—continued.			
bóc,	boc,	boke,	book.
mete,	met,	mete,	mete.
fét,	fet,	fete,	feet.
slæp,	slep,	slepe,	sleep.
stém,	stem,	steme,	steam.
sprécan,	sprekenn,	speke,	speak.

This table shows that the long sound in A.S. was denoted by the accent, its absence indicating the short. In the Early English of the Ormulum the long was denoted by a single consonant, the short by a double; in Middle English the long by a final *e mute*, the short by its absence—all these expedients, except the accent, being employed in modern English, besides many others, most capriciously. Thus long *e* by *e mute* in *mete*, *ee* in *feet*, *ea* in *steam*; long *o* by *e mute* in *bone*, *oa* in *oath*, *oo* in *good*, with a change of pronunciation (See Section V. § 63).

SPECIMENS—ORMULUM.

58. The following short extract will serve further to illustrate the method pursued in the Ormulum, just explained:—

ORMULUM, 1220—1250.

I hafe set here o[1] thiss boc amang Godspelles[2] wordes
Alle thruh meselfen manigword the rime swa to fillen ;[3]
Acc[1] thu shal finden[3] that minn word eggwhaer[5] thœr[15] it is ekedd[6]
Magg[7] helpen[3] tha[8] thatt reden[3] it to sen[3] and understanden ;[3]
All thess[9] to bettre hu thegm[10] buth[11] the Godspell understanden ;[3]
And for[12] the trowwe[13] icc thatt te birrth[11] wel tholenn[14] mine wordes
Eggwhaer[5] thaer[15] thu shalt finden[3] him amang Godspelles[2] wordes.

1=on=in. 2=Gospel's, full genitive in *es*. 3=to fill, to complete ; inf. in *en* prevailing throughout this and the next period. 4=but, A.S. 5=everywhere. 6=added, cf., A.S. *eác*. 7=may, A.S. *mœg*. 8=those, A.S. 9=all the better how. 10=them ; a mixture of A.S. *heom* and Engl. *them*. 11=it becomes. 12=for that=therefore. 13=I trow. 14=to hear. 15=where, A.S.

The style is so very modern that it is hoped these few notes may be sufficient to render the whole perfectly intelligible. The metre is what has been called long Iambic, consisting of not less than fourteen nor more than fifteen syllables, with a break or cæsura at the end of the eighth.*

Next to the Ormulum, the most important works of this age are perhaps the Rhyming Chronicles of Robert of Gloucester, and of Robert Mannyng, of Brunne, to the former of whom is also attributed a voluminous collection of the lives of the principal saints in the calendar. The language is more modern than that of the Ormulum, composed probably about the year 1300 or a little later. Here is an extract from the life of St. Patrick, containing an allusion to a famous national tradition :—

Seyn Pateryk com thoru Godes grace to preche in Irelonde,
To teche men ther¹ ryt believe Jesu Cryste to understonde :²
So ful of wormes³ that londe he founde that no man ni myghte gon,²
In some stede⁴ for worms³ that he nas wenemyd⁶ anon ;
Seynt Pateryk bade our Lorde Cryst that the londe delyvered were,
Of thilke foule wormis³ that none ne com there.

1 = *th* for *h*, but not for the first time in the plural of the 3 pers. pronoun : *ther* and *their* for *heoru, hira, hir ; theom* and *them* for *heom, him ; they* for *hi*, tho' not fully established in the Southern dialect until modern times (see Sec. VI., § 89). 2 = the final *n* of inf. has already become a matter of convenience. It is dropped or retained according to the exigencies of the rhyme. 3 = three forms of the pl. strong, weak, and modern : *wormis, wormes, worms*. 4 = places, cf. *stead*. 5 = ne was = was not. 6 = wounded. Here are only two new Norman terms, *grace* and *delyvered*.

The next is from an ode on Heaven, Death, and Judgment, which may have been written about the same time as the foregoing, though Warton refers it, with a vast amount of poetry of the same age, 1280–1320, to the twelfth century (Hist. Engl. Poetry, I. 33). The *alliteration* is sustained throughout very regularly :—

* On the versification of the Ormulum, which seems to have been composed in imitation of a Latin rhythm, Marsh remarks that it 'differs from the Anglo-Saxon models in wanting alliteration, and in possessing a regular metrical flow ; from the Norman French in wanting rhyme ; and, allowing for the difference between accent and classical quantity, it closely resembles that of some Latin poems of the Middle Ages, from which it was probably imitated.'—*English Language*, p. 179.

Alliterative Ode—1300 (?).

Middel-erd for mon was mad,
Unmighti aren is meste mede,
This hedy hath on honde yhad,
That hevene hem is haste to hede.
Ich erde a blisse budel us bade,   *That he ben derne done.*
The dreri domesdai to drede
Of sinful sauhting sone be sad,
That derne doth this derne dede,
This wrakefall werkes under wede,
    In soule soteleth sone.

Rhyme began to be now universally employed, instead of the old measure, especially by the so-called rhyming chroniclers, who translated from the French. Its introduction must be attributed to Norman influence, though it was known from the remotest times, and used by the Saxons, especially in their Latin compositions. A good specimen is afforded by a ballad written in the year 1301, on the occasion of a defeat sustained by the French under the Count of Artois, at the hands of the revolted Flemings :—

Susteneth lordinges, bothe zonge* and olde,
Of the Frynsche men that were so proude ante bolde,
How the Flemmyshe men bohten hem and solde,
    Upon a Wednesday.
Betere hem were at home in huere londe,
Than force seche Flemishe bi the sea stronde,
Whare souch moni Frensh wyf wryngeth hire honde,
    And syngeth welaway.

---

* With regard to this form *zonge* for young, it should be observed that ʒ is used here as elsewhere, simply to represent a letter similar to it in form, constantly occurring in old MSS., which, however, never was pronounced like *z*, but always either as *g* or *y*, according to the period and dialect in question. By this time, that is towards the close of the thirteenth century, the Saxon *g* had mostly become *y* in the Southern dialects; we should here therefore read *young* as in modern English. At an earlier stage of the language it would have been *geong*, though the tendency to soften this letter had already made its appearance even in Saxon times, as is evident by such forms as mæniu for mænigu = many; iogoð for geoguð = youth, occasionally to be met with in old MSS.

The Kynge of Ffrance made statutes newe,
In the londe of Flaunders among false and **trewe**,
That the communs of Bruges ful sore can arewe,
    And seiden among hem,
Gedere we us togedere hardilyche at ene,
Take we the bailifs by twenty and by tene,
Clappe we of the hevedes an oven o the grene
    And cast we in the fen.

ROBERT MANNYNG.

59. The next is a characteristic specimen of the style of Robert Mannyng, a writer whose merits and real position have scarcely yet been sufficiently recognised. His language is greatly in advance not only of his contemporaries, but even of most writers of the next, or Chaucerian period. The reason is that it was his constant endeavour, as he in many places tells us, to write for the people in the plain, simple style of the spoken language, which we have already seen was always in advance of the literary standard. Hence, though he writes at the very beginning of the fourteenth century, he is much easier and more intelligible than perhaps any writer of the following generation. He thus occupies a somewhat exceptional position in the history of the language, and may truly be said to be the first author that wrote readable English.

The passage occurs in the prologue to his Chronicle. which he appears to have finished before the year 1338 :—

    Lordynges, that be now here,
    If ze will listene and lere
    All þe story of Inglande
    Als Robert Mannyng writen it fand,
    And in Inglisch has it shewed,
    Not for þe lerid bot for þe lewed, (ignorant)
    For þo þat in j is land wonn,
    Þat þe Latyn no Frankis conn
    For to have solace and gamen.
    In felawschip when þai sitt samen **(together)**

>   . . . . . .
> Þai sayd in so quainte Inglis,
> Þat mony one wate not what it is,
> And forsoth I couth noght
> So strange Inglis as þai wroght,
> And men besoght me many a tyme,
> To turn it bot in light ryme,
> And þerfore for þe comonaltie
> Þat blyþely wild listen to me,
> On light lange I it began
> For luf of þe lewed man . . .
> Of Brunne I am, if any me blame
> Robert Mannyng is my name . . .
> In the þrid Edward's tyme was I
> When I wrote alle þis story.

Mannyng is also the author of a curious work, which he calls the 'Handlyng Synne,' partly translated from William of Waddington's 'Manuel des Pechiez,' and the date of which is fixed by himself:—

> 'Dane Filip was master that time
> That I began this English rime,
> The yere of grace fell then to be
> A thousand three hundred and three.'

It may be observed that his vocabulary is marked by a large accession of Romance terms, and that his grammar is rendered very modern by the substitution of *s* for *th* in the 3rd pers. sing., and of *scho, thei, ther,* for the older forms *seo, hi, heora.*

We shall close this section with an extract from an elegy on the death of Edward I., 1307, which reads quite English :—

> 'The messager to the Pope com,
> And seyde that our kynge was dede,
> Ys own honde the lettre he nom (took),
> Y wis his herte wes ful gret :
> The Pope himself the lettre redde,
> And spec a word of gret honour :
> "Alas !" he said, " is Edward ded ?
> Of Cristendome he ben the flour !"

Grammar of the Transition Period.   89

> 'The Pope is to chaumbre wende,
> For dole nemihte he speke na more;
> And after cardinales he sende
> That much conthen of Cristes lore.
> Both the lasse ant eke the more,
> Bed hem both red and synge;
> Gret deol me myhte se thore (there)
> Mony mon is honde wrynge.'

Our limited space compels the omission of a document exceedingly interesting in the history of the language: the Proclamation of Henry III., in 1258, to the People of Huntingdon, considered one of the earliest extant specimens of what may be called *English*, as opposed to Semi-Saxon:—
'Henr', thurg Godes fultome (help) king on Engleneloande, Lhoauerd on Yreloand, Duk on Norm' on Aquitain' and Eorl on Aniow, send gretinge to alle hise halde, *ilaerde and ilawed* (learned and unlearned, or *lay*), on Huntendon' schir,' etc.

SUPPLEMENT TO THE GRAMMAR OF THE TRANSITION PERIOD.

The subjoined summary, embodying the conclusions hitherto arrived at, is condensed from a paper on the subject contributed by Dr. Morris to C. W. Hazlitt's annotated edition of 'Warton's History of English Poetry,' London, 1871, Vol. II. pp. 25-7.

CHANGES FROM 1100 TO 1150.

Mostly orthographical.

1. The endings *a*, *o*, *u* reduced to *e*, affecting all the cases of noun and adjective, and causing great confusion, the endings

an		
um		en
ena		
on	becoming	
as		es
ath		eth
rá, ru		re
od, ode		ed, ede

2. *C* sometimes softened to *ch*, and *g* to *y* or *i*, but *sc* remains unchanged.

3. *N* often added to final *e*, and *n* often dropped, especially in the *n* declension, and the definite declension of adj

CHANGES FROM 1150 TO 1250.

Great grammatical changes, and the orthographical ones fully established.

1. The indef. article *an* (*a*) grows out of the numeral *an* (*one*), retaining most of its older endings.

2. The def. article *se*, *seo*, *that* changed for *the*, *theo*, *thet* (*that*), with a tendency to use an uninflected *the*, even in the pl., for *tha* or *tho*.

3. Pl. of nouns in *a* or *u* change to *en* or *e*.

4. Gen. pl. *es* occasionally for *e* or *ene*; and the pl. *es* often for *en*.

5. Gender of nouns confused.

6. The gen. sing. mas. of the indef. adj. and the gen. and dat. fem. of the def. tend to disappear.

7. Dual forms still occur, but less frequently.

8. New Pronominal forms spring up:

    ha, *a* = he, she, they ; is (hise) = *hire* = *her*.
    his, *is* = *hi*, *heo* = them ; *me* = men = man = Fr. *on*.

That is used as an indeclinable relative both for the indeclinable *the* and for *se*, *seo*.

    Which, *whose*, *whom*, *what*, come in as relatives.

9. The *n* of *min*, *thin* dropped before consonants, but retained in the oblique case.

10. The gen. cases of the pronouns are becoming mere possessives: *mi-self*, *thi-self* for *me self*, *the self*.

11. Inf. *n* frequently dropped: smelle = smellen ; and often takes *to* as in the first text of Layamon.

12. The gerundial or dat. inf. becomes *en* or *e* for *ene* = *enne*, *anne*.

13. *N* of passive part. often dropped: *icume* = *icumen* = *come*.

14. Pres. part. in *inde* for *ende*, and is often used for the dat. inf.: *to swimende* = *to swimene* = to swim. This corruption is found even before 1066.

15. *Shall* and *will* are used as future auxiliaries. The above changes refer to the Southern dialect. But the *Ormulum* [East Midland] has a general disregard for nearly all inflexions. Thus, the art. is uninflected in the sing., and in the pl. the nom. *tha* only occurs. *That* is a demonstrative and not the neuter of the art. Gender much as in

Grammar of the Transition Period.

modern English. Gen. in *s* used for mas. and fem. nouns. *Thezz, thezzre, thezzm* for *hi, heore, heom, zho = she* for *heo*. Verbal pl. in *en* for *eth*, except imperative ; *i* or *ge* of passive part. dropped. The 2nd pers. past. of strong verbs often loses its ending.

The *Ancren Riwle*, *St. Marharete*, &c., have *sch* for *sc*, a change which seems to have taken place after 1200.

In these latter works there is a mixture of dialect, and a simpler grammatical structure than in Layamon, &c.

Arn occurs, as in the *Ormulum*, for *beoth* or *sind*.

Changes from 1250 to 1300.

1. Gen. sing. and acc. mas. of def. art. not wholly lost in Southern dialect ; *tho* is the pl. of all cases.

2. Gender of nouns much simplified, owing to loss of adjectival endings.

3. Pl. of nouns in *en* and *es* are used indiscriminately.

4. Gen. in *es* becomes more general, often taking the place of the older *en* or *e* (*n* decl.), of *e* (fem. nouns) and of the pl. *ene* or *e*.

5. Dat. *e* sing. and pl. often dropped.

6. Dual forms rare, disappearing before 1300.

7. Adjectival endings reduced to *e*. But the gen. pl. *re* retained in few cases, as *al-re*, as well as the gen. sing. *es* in a few pronominal forms, as *eaches, otheres*.

8. The gerundial inf. in *e* or *en* more common than in *ene*.

9. Some strong verbs become weak.

10. Pres. part. in *inge* appears in second text of Layamon, say 1270.

All these points are subject to occasional exceptions caused by dialectical differences. Thus, the Kentish of the thirteenth century, as far as we know it, has older forms than the Western, as seen in Layamon, as *se = the*, mas. *si* = fem., &c. ; while the *Ayenbite* of the fourteenth century is more inflexional in many respects than the *Ancren Riwle* and *St. Marharete*.

QUESTIONS.

46. What process distinguishes Old E. from Semi-Saxon ? How is Old English subdivided ? Extent of Early E. ?

47. How did the union of the two races consequent on the separation of England from the mainland affect the language at first ?

48. What change took place in the alphabet ? How did this affect the orthography ?

49. What three languages were used at this time in literature? Why may this be considered a fortunate circumstance?

50. What species of composition exhibits the language in the most forward state? Why? What is the chief difference between the grammar of Semi-Saxon and Early English? What great change did this necessitate?

51. How was the general softening of the A.S. inflexions effected? This is important in scansion? *He loves, we, ye, they love*, in Early English?

52. Mention some other changes. Are these uniform? What is the origin of our infinitive? How far is it a real mood? How is the change of A.S. active participle in *-ende* to *-ing* explained? Are all our words in *-ing* necessarily active participles? 'He forbiddis al discord in *teaching, sayand* let na scismes be amang you.' Parse the two words in Italics.

53. Show from the words *heom* and *þare* in the *transition table*, that the case-endings, even when retained, had already lost their *force* and *significance*. *Singað* explains why the termination *th* or *eth* in verbs was plural, not only singular, as now?

54. What is the general state of the vocabulary? How far is the Ormulum affected by Normanisms? Mention certain *classes* of French words introduced into the spoken language by this time, and account for this on historical grounds, and give instances.

55. Is *one* or *six* from the Latin *unus* and *sex*, or from the A.S. *án* and *six*? *Eight* from A.S. *eahta*, or French *huit*? Why is it sometimes difficult to say whether a word is A.S. or Romance in its origin? What rule is to be observed? In comparative philology, what principle, if attended to, will prevent false and absurd *derivations*?

56. Give an account of the Ormulum. Its date, etc. Its language as compared with that of Layamon.

57. In what does the chief peculiarity of its *orthography* consist? How is this a clue to the *pronunciation* of the day? Did its orthographic system prevail to any extent? Mention the different expedients employed in Saxon, Early, Middle, and Modern English times, to denote the length of the vowels.

59. What position does Robert Mannyng occupy in the history of the language? Mention his principal works and the chief peculiarities of his grammar and vocabulary.

SECTION V.

(1350-1450.)

MIDDLE ENGLISH PERIOD—FURTHER DEVELOPMENT—STATE OF THE GRAMMAR—VOCABULARY—NORMAN ELEMENT—CAUSE OF ITS LATE INTRODUCTION—SPECIMENS—BARBOUR—DOUGLAS—ACCOUNT OF THE SCOTCH DIALECT.

MIDDLE ENGLISH PERIOD—ITS EXTENT.

60. So far as the structure of the language is concerned, there is no essential difference between this period and the foregoing. They are both comprised under the one name of *Old English*, and have been divided into the *Early* and *Middle* English Periods, in order to analyze more accurately the steps by which the transition was effected from Broken Saxon to Modern English. Though generally described as a period of *reconstruction*, it was, in reality, one of further *dissolution;* or, in other words, the process by which the language was moulded into its present shape, was what might be called a process of *elimination*, a continual softening down and eliding of the old grammatical inflexions, which, if allowed to proceed far enough, would have resulted in a speech as nearly as possible perfectly analytic. So long as this tendency to simplicity of structure is actively at work, we are in the transition stage; as soon as it ceases, or is arrested at a certain state, we reach the Modern or Fixed Period of the language. This state was arrived at about the year 1450, after which time the language sustained no further loss of grammatical forms. All, or nearly all, the inflexions that it possessed then, it still retains. That date, therefore, marks the time when the process of reconstruction was complete, leaving an extent of about one hundred years to the Present or Middle English Period, 1350–1450.

DIFFERENCE BETWEEN THE EARLY AND MIDDLE ENGLISH PERIODS.

61. The difficulty of distinguishing between one stage and another increases in proportion as the real difference diminishes. So long as we have to deal with bold landmarks, standing prominently forward, we are enabled by their presence or absence to trace and point out the changes that the language has undergone from time to time. But when these become weakened or effaced, the minor differences that still exist, and by which alone we can draw a line between two periods, are very apt to escape our notice and pass without observation. This is the difficulty that immediately arises when we set about comparing the present with the foregoing period, and it is increased by the fact that many grammatical forms which are considered peculiarly characteristic of Early English, are constantly occurring in the Middle English Period.* The last circumstance, however, gives us the clue to what must be considered the only essential difference between the two, viz., that *inflexions still kept up, and which in the former preserved a certain innate force and significance, have in the latter lost their true meaning and import.* Heom or hom may occasionally, in Old English, have its full dative force without further aid; in Middle English hardly ever, if used at all, without the addition of the relational *to: to hom.* So the final *e* in *alle* may convey a plural meaning in the *one;* in the *other* it is devoid of such power. Hence the grammatical forms of Middle English are not *distinguishing* terminations, being useless as guides to the sense of a passage, and requiring the

---

* The writings of Robert Mannyng, noticed in the last section, prove that the converse of this is also true.

addition of the relational words, just as much as if they were not employed; they are different ways of writing a word, availed of as a great convenience by the poets of the time, in the same way as Homer turned to account the unsettled state of the Greek language when he wrote. Chaucer uses or drops, as best suits his purpose, the proper infinitive and other terminations that still lingered in the language: 'that it was may *me thoughten* tho'' (then); and further on: '*methought* one night in my sleeping'; 'women desyren to *have* soveraynte'; and 'he was worthy *han* his lyfe'; *to sain* and *to say, to maken* and *to maké, to seen* and *to see, youngé* (plur.) and *young, tho thinges* and *those things, gone* and *y-gone, he told* and *he y-told*, where the past *participle* suffix *y=ge* A.S. has so far lost its true import, that it is actually transferred to the past *tense* for the sake of the metre. The consequence was that, later on, when it was thought desirable to give the language a certain uniformity, all these double forms were felt to be an incumbrance, and, the tendency being towards simplicity, the older and more complicate were doomed, and very soon disappeared altogether.

FINAL e—WHEN PRONOUNCED.

62. The final *e*, which in Early English served for such a variety of purposes, and was, perhaps, never mute before a consonant, having now become quite meaningless, is often not pronounced as a distinct syllable, and only retained in writing as it is to this day. In Chaucer sometimes it forms a syllable, sometimes it does not; and the difficulty of determining when it should be pronounced, or not, has occasioned much doubt and difference of opinion as to the real nature of his poetic system. Some hold that it is regulated by the *accent* alone, as is Christabel and some of Walter Scott's poetry; others that it is strictly syllabic, of the same nature as, and the true origin of, our heroic measure. The latter is now the generally received opinion, and is adopted by Tyrwhitt, to whom we owe the first fairly correct edition of the 'Canterbury Tales' (1775). He supposes that Chaucer borrowed it from the Italians, and observes that, as with them, it is generally endecasyllabic, occasionally extended to twelve syllables (endecasillabo sdrucciolo), sometimes limited to ten (endecasillabo tronco), as it nearly always is in the modern heroic system. The two, however, are so far identical that the *accent* in both is the same, falling regularly on the even syllable, the tenth being the last accented in all cases. The final *e* in Chaucer is usually said to constitute a distinct syllable, when it stands for any of *the old endings*, for the *French e* at that time pronounced, or is *adverbial*, provided always the following word begin with a consonant. It would be, perhaps, better to say, that in these instances, it has or has not syllabic force, according to the requirements of the metre, to which accent, grammar, and pronunciation are generally made subservient by the Middle English poets.

FINAL *e* FRENCH—ACCENT.

63. With regard to the *e* French (called *e* feminine), it seems quite certain that the new words retained for some time both their proper accent and pronunciation, only gradually conforming themselves to the genius of the English tongue. In this the tendency, we have seen, was to throw the accent as far back as possible, in French to throw it forward. Hence Chaucer constantly varies the accent of many new terms to suit his purpose, as: *langudgĕ* and *linguage, natŭre* and *nătŭre, virtue* and *virtŭe, commandĕ-ment* and *commándement, contraíre* and *cóntraire, couràge, pilgrimàge*, etc. As soon as the accent was permanently shifted, the final *e* ceased to be pronounced, and the word became thoroughly *Anglicised*. Perhaps it was this French practice that occasioned a remarkable license, observable especially in ballad poetry down to recent times, of varying the accent even of Saxon words at pleasure: *ladỳ, harpèr, singèr, mornìng, singìng*.

GRAMMATICAL AND ORTHOGRAPHIC VALUE OF FINAL e.

64. The old endings, now universally represented by the final *e* syllabic, are principally, in *nouns*, the dative singular and genitive plural; in *adjectives*, the plural; and in *verbs*, the 1st and 3rd person singular of the present and past tenses; besides, a further weakened form of the infinitive, *givé*, *lové*, *také*, for *given*, *loven*, *taken*. Mr. Guest has even shown that in some instances, though very rarely, final *e* preserves its full inflexional force, without the aid of separate particles or relational words. Thus

'Hire greatest othé n'as but by Seint Loy' (Chaucer)

is equivalent to: her greatest *of oathes*, the *e* of *othé* being = A.S. gen. plur. *a*, *otha* of oathes. In

'The drought of March had perced to the *roté*' (Chaucer),

roté = dat. sing. of *rot* = root, here, however, with the addition of the dat. particle *to*.

'Pouré menné cotes' ('Piers Ploughman's Vision'),

stands for '*poor mens*' cots,' and

'her horsé knave' (Gower's 'Confessio Amantis'),

for their horse's groom. The *adverbial* force of the final *e* seems to occur only in the *positive* degree, *swifte* = swiftly, *firste* = firstly.

'And in a cloth of gold that *brighté* shone' (Chaucer),

where *brighte* = *brightly*. This adverbial form explains the constant use, in the most classic writers, of what appears to be the adjective instead of the adverb. It is, in reality, the Old English adverb, with the final *e* first dropped in pronunciation, and then in writing.

'*Soft* went the music the soft air along' (Keats).

In the superlative the adverb terminated in *-est* simply, as in A.S. *swiftost* and *swiftest* = Old English *swiftest* = modern *swiftliest*. So *brightest* = *brightliest*, adv.; but *brighteste* = *brightest*, adj. The final *e mute* is believed now, for the first time, to have been extensively employed by those of the Norman school of writing as an orthographic expedient to lengthen the preceding vowel. This purpose was effected in A.S. times by the *accent;* but this having been abolished with the old alphabet, a new method was required: A.S. *gód* = Old English *gode* = *good;* *fúl* = *fole* = *foul;* *gés* = *gese* = *gees;* *blód* = *blode* = *blood;* *hús* = *hose* = *house;* *fót* = *fote* = *foot;* *lif* = *life* = *life*, etc. From these examples it appears that, if we suppose the pronunciation of an A.S. *accented* vowel to be uniform, as great a change has taken place in the pronunciation of the language as in its orthographic system (see Sec. IV. § 57).

MIDDLE ENGLISH NOUN—POSSESSIVE—PLURAL.

65. The total disappearance of the final *e syllabic*, or rather of its functions (to include both the written and spoken language), constitutes, perhaps, the greatest, though not the most striking, difference between Middle and Modern English.

Other grammatical forms, peculiar to this period, were the following:—

In the *noun* the possessive and plural endings were alike, as now, but often made a complete syllable, as *thingés* = thing's and *things, werkés* = *works, bankés, Goddés sake, wordés, frerés*. Attention to this is of great assistance in reading Chaucer:—

> 'But preacheth not as frerés don in Lent
> To make us for our oldé sinnés weep,'

when read as here accented, are two perfect heroic lines. A fuller plural in *-is* sometimes occurs: *to make bokis, songis*, and *ditis* (*Chaucer*). Many plurals in *en* were also retained, some of which have survived to our time: *shoon, eyen, bischopen, eldren, arwen, doghtren, sustren, unclen, treen, hosen, chicken* (?), *oxen, toen, tone,* and *ton.* The syllable in A.S. was *an,* the universal pl. of nouns of the simple order: *eagan=eyen=eyes, tan=toen=toes;* but we shall see that the greater number of the Old English plurals in *-en* are not accounted for by reference to this A.S. declension (Sec. VI., § 87).

PRONOUN—INFINITIVE—PAST PARTICIPLE.

66. In the *pronoun,* the forms *I, ich,* and *iche* occur. It is not the only instance of a mixture of archaic and modern forms, the middle state naturally participating of, and connecting the stages immediately preceding and following it. So *hi* and *they, ye* and *you,* the latter nearly always accusative. This distinction may have caused it subsequently to be used singularly in the spoken language: *hir, hire* and *their, hire* and *her, hire* being invariably a monosyllable; *hem* (as modern *'em*) and *them* (see Sec. VI., § 90).

In the *verb* the infinitive was in *-en, with a tendency to drop the n,* eliding the final *e* before a vowel. We find *to haen=to han=to havé=to hav'(e), specan=speken=speké, maken=maké* and (in the last line cited) *mak'(e).* What was at first done for euphony sake became later on the universal practice in the *spoken* language, sometimes without further change, sometimes with a compensative lengthening of the root vowel. We say *hăv(e), gĭv(e), lŏv(e),* but *tāk(e), māk(e), dō* (for *dŏn*), *bē* (for *bĕn*).

The *past participle,* according to the writer's fancy or convenience, drops the old A.S. suffix *ge,* now softened into *y: ytaught, ymaked, ybroken, ysought, ysowen, ycleped,* but also *cleped, maked,* etc. It is common enough in Spenser, who was fond of archaic forms: *ydrad=dreaded, ypight= fixed, ywrote, ybore, ytold,* etc.; and even in so late a writer as Thomson:—

'Yet all these sounds *yblent* inclined all to sleep'—
'But these his talents were *yburied* stark'—

'*ypricked* deep'—'from Heaven this life *ysprung*'—'*yborn* to rise,' etc., in the 'Castle of Indolence.'

PRESENT INDICATIVE.

67. The *present indicative* is now generally sing., *lové, lovest, loveth;* plural, *we, ye, they loven*, instead of *loveth*, as in Early English (see last sec., § 6). Trevisa, the translator of Higden's 'Polychronicon' (1385), still retains the old form: 'other naciouns *beth*'=ben=be=are; 'thei *cunneth*'=connen=can; thei *lerneth, leveth, haveth*, etc. This is, of course, the proper pl. ending from A.S. *að*=*ath*=*eth*, *we bringað*=we bringath=we bringeth. How the infinitive *-en*, *bringen, singen, loven*, was now substituted for it has not been explained. The modern Greeks, in much the same way, say εἶναι for ἐστί. The practice prevailed very generally, Ben Jonson tells us in his English Grammar, 'till about the reign of Henry VIII. . . . thus *loven, sayen, complainen*. But now (whatsoever is the cause) it hath quite grown out of use, and that other so generally prevailed, that I dare not presume to set this afoot again, albeit (to tell you my opinion) I am persuaded that the lack thereof, well considered, will be found a great blemish in our tongue. For seeing *time* and *person* be, as it were, the right and left hand of a verb, what can the maiming bring else but a lameness to the whole body?' He was not aware that this *lameness* already existed in A.S. times, and may be the reason why our first pers. sing. and the plural are alike. They said *ic lufige* and *lufige we*, as well as *we lufiað, I love, we love; ic bærne, we, ge, hi bærnað*, and *bærne, we, ge, hi*, I, we, you, they *burn*. For a similar reason the third per. sing. and the pl. were identical in *Early English: he loveth, we loveth*. The A.S. *að* and *ð* of the third pers., and *iað* and *að* pl., were in both case⁻

softened into *ath* and then *eth*: *he bærnð, we bærnað; he lufað, we lufað*, becoming *he bernath, we bernath, he burneth, we burneth; he, we lovath* and *loveth*, etc. Perhaps this may account for the substitution in *Middle English* of the infinitive *en* in the plural, to distinguish it from the third sing.: *he burneth, we burnen.** As a synthetic language decays, certain grammatical forms are very liable to get confused, thus occasioning a further change to avoid ambiguity. The Latin imperfect *amabam* becoming *amava* and *amavo* in Italian, the future *amabo*, when softened also into *amavo*, was no longer distinguishable from it. This identity necessitated some new form for one or other of these tenses, and actually originated the modern Italian † future system: *amare ho=amar-o=amerò, amare hai= amar-ai=amerai, amare ha=amar-a = amerà*, etc., as we say sometimes, *I have to do* so and so, instead of *I must* or *shall.*

PAST TENSE—IMPERATIVE.

68. The *past tense* makes both *ede* and *ed*, *edest* and *edst*, *ede* and *ed* in the sing., *ed* and *eden* in the pl., *ed* being always a full syllable: I and he *lovéde* and *lovéd, thou lovédest* and *lovedst;* we, ye, they *lovéd* and *lovéden*, and occasionally *lovedeth*, against all analogy, as the A.S. form is: *ic* and *he lufode, pú lufodest; we, ge, hi lufoden* and

---

* The substitution first took place in the *Midland* dialect, and thence gradually spread South, where it supplanted *eth*, and North, where it supplanted *es*. 'A special peculiarity of this [the West-Midland] dialect, and which distinguishes it from the Southern and Northumbrian, is that of the inflexions of the plural in the present indicative mood; in the Southern dialect it is *eth*, in the Northumbrian *es*, in the Midland *en*, and this termination is found to be employed systematically throughout these poems.' Notice of 'Early English Alliterative Poems, edited by R. Morris, 1864,' in 'Westminster Review' for April, 1865.

† This is true also of the French, Spanish, and other Romance tongues, showing that the tendency towards this change must have already existed in classical times.

lufedon, never *lufodað*. Instances of the double form are: they *cried* and *crieden*, *were* and *weren*, *mote* and *moten* (*must*), *might* and *mighten:* 'his ton toteden out' (his toes peeped out); 'his hosen overhongen,' etc. ('Piers Ploughman's Creed').

The imperative second pers. sing. and pl. is generally in *eth* and *th*, from the Early English: *lovath ye*=*loveth ye*, and sometimes *lové ye*.

> 'Now *telleth* ye sire monk, if that ye conne' (Chaucer),
> '*Riseth* up, sir preest, and *stondeth* by me' (Ditto).

Beth still=*be still*, *witteth*=*know ye*, *goth*=*go ye*, *taketh*=*take ye*, *cometh*=*come ye*, etc. Little trace remains of the *subjunctive* or *gerund*.

HELP VERBS—TO HAVE, TO BE, SHALL, WILL, &c.

69. *To have* was conjugated in accordance with the foregoing forms: indicative pres., I *have*, thou *havest* and *hast*, he *haveth* and *hath;* plur. *haven*, *haen* and *han;* past, I and he *hadde*, thou *haddest;* plur. *hadden;* infinitive, to *haven*, to *haen* and to *han;* imperative, *haveth*, *haveth* ye. *To be* made: *am*, *art*, *is;* plur. *aren* and *ben*, *weren* and *were;* imperative, *beth;* inf. *to ben*. The other auxiliaries varied considerably: *may*, *mow*, plur. *mowen;* past, *mighte*, *might*, *moughte;* plur. *mighten*, *moughten;* *can*, *con;* plur. *connen*, *conne;* past, *coude*, *couden*, *couthen*. The *l* was introduced later on into this tense *could*, by apparent analogy with *would*, *should*, and disregard of its true origin. *Will*, *wil*, *wol*, *willen*, *wollen;* past, *wolde*, *wolden*. *Shal*, *shall*, plur. *shull;* past, *shulde*, *shulden*. These two verbs were now universally used as they are at present, with the infinitive to form the future. As *shall* originally implied *obligation*, it had a natural reference to future time; and as the obligation we impose on *ourselves* is lighter than that we impose on others, it must clearly have a stronger meaning in the second and third person than in the first: *I shall go=I must go* (originally), *thou shalt not go=thou must not go*. Again, as *will* meant *resolution, determination*, it also had reference to future time (cf. modern Greek θέλω ἀγαπᾷν=ἀγαπήσω); and as the resolution we form for ourselves must necessarily be stronger than that we announce of others, *will*, in the first person, must be more emphatic than in the second and third, *I will go* than *thou wilt go*, etc. Here is the whole mystery explained by reference to the original meaning of these words: *scealan=to owe* a thing, *willan=to will* a thing.

GERUND AND MODERN INFINITIVE.

70. All these verbs were used in A.S. as auxiliaries always with the *infinitive*, never with the *gerund*, except in a passive sense, as: *is eác tó witanne=it is also to be known; ic sceal macian*, not: *ic sceal tó macigenne (I shall make); we sceolon gecláensian=we must cleanse; beón wolde=would be; nú mage we secgan=now may we say; heó hit ne mæg his gewittes bereáfian=she cannot bereave it of its wits*. The *gerund*, we have seen, was a sort of dative case of the infinitive, with the particle *tó* always prefixed: *tó lufigenne, tó habbenne, tó lærenne (teach); tó lybbenne*. This particle never was used with the *proper infinitive: lufian*, not *tó lufian, habban, læran, lybban;* consequently it cannot be employed in Modern English with the auxiliaries: *I may teach*, not *I may to teach, we can say, they should love*, etc. Such expressions, therefore, are not different *moods* of the verb, any more than would be the corresponding A.S. *ic mæg læran*, etc. In them alone do we find traces of a real infinitive, simply because the A.S. auxiliaries governed the verb in the infinitive mood; all others take the particle *to*, which is not the sign of the *infinitive proper*, but of its dative case or *gerund*. In order to avoid repetition in the next section, the grammar of this period has been treated as well with reference to the modern as to the previous stages of the language.

PROCLAMATION OF EDWARD III.—RECOGNITION OF ENGLISH AS THE NATIONAL SPEECH.

71. In the year 1362, 36th of Edward III., it was enacted by statute that the English *might be* now substituted for the Norman tongue, hitherto employed exclusively in all public acts and judicial proceedings. 'The proceedings were all written, as indeed all public proceedings were, in Norman or Law French, and even the arguments of the counsel and the decisions of the court were in the same barbarous dialect. This continued till the reign of Edward III., who having employed his arms successfully in subduing the crown of France, thought it unbecoming the dignity of the victors to use any longer the language of a vanquished country. By a statute, therefore, passed in the 36th year of his reign (1362), it was enacted that for the future all pleas *should be* pleaded, shown, defended, answered, debated, and judged in the English tongue, but be entered and enrolled in Latin' (Blackstone, iii. 21), where the great lawyer exhibits more zeal and patriotic feeling than historic accuracy. It appears that the decree referred to only so far tolerated the E. language as to *allow* it to be used in the courts, not by any means to the exclusion of the rival tongue. Of course this was a great step, and quite sufficient to secure the ultimate ascendancy of the language of the masses. In fact the statute itself was necessitated by the growing importance of the latter, rather than dictated by jealousy of the former. At the same time it was decreed that no clergyman, ignorant of English, should be promoted to any preferment or benefice, because the great body of the people spoke no other language. This is the first legal recognition of English as the language of the country, and is a great landmark in its history. It points out the time when French had ceased to be spoken outside the court and the upper house, and when the native speech had recovered its ascendancy. French had been falling off since the beginning of the century, and when, owing to the separation of England from the mainland, it became a corrupt dialect, very different from that spoken in Paris, it ceased to be any longer used in literature. Chaucer, in several places, sneers at the French current in the country in his time, and ridicules all who still endeavoured to employ it in conversation or writing. The Prioress in the 'Canterbury Tales' spoke French fluently enough, but

> 'After the scole of Stratford atté Bowe,
> For *Frenche of Paris was to hire unknowe.*'

And in the prologue to his 'Testament of Love' he says: 'Certes, there ben some that speke thyr poysy mater in French, of whyche speeche the Frenche men have as good a fantasye as we have in hearing of Frenche mennes Englische.' Further on he recommends the *clerks*, or clergy, to 'endyten in Latyn, for they have the propertye in science and the knowinge in that facultye, and lette Frenche men in theyr Frenche also endyte theyr queynt termes, for it is kyndly (natural) to theyr mouthes; and lette us shewe our fantasyes in such wordes *as we learneden of our dames tonge.*' It is not a little remarkable that his contemporary, Gower (1324—1408), composed in all three of these languages. His 'Vox Clamantis,' which has never been printed, is in *Latin;* his 'Speculum Meditantis,' now lost, together with fifty *balades,* or sonnets, was in *French;* and his 'Confessio Amantis,' his best known work, is in English. He even excuses himself for any mistakes he may have committed in his French compositions, on the plea that he wrote in a foreign idiom:—

> 'Et si ieo n'ai de François la faconde,
> Pardonetz moi qe ieo de ceo forsvoie.
> Jeo sui Englois.'

He was probably the last Englishman that employed French in any serious *literary* work. English remained ever after without a rival in the world of letters.

LATE INTRODUCTION OF NORMAN WORDS.

72. And yet not till this time was its vocabulary affected to any extent by Normanisms. French was for 300 years (1066—1362) politically the language of the country, spoken and written almost exclusively by the upper classes, and alone used as a medium of instruction. 'Children in scole, agenes the usage and maner of alle other naciouns, beth compelled for to leve her owne language, and for to constrewe her lessouns and her thingis *a Frensche*, and haveth siththe (since) that the Normans come first into England. Also gentil mennes children beth ytaugnt for to speke Frensche from the time that thei beth rokked in her cradel, and kunneth speke and playe with a childes brooche. And uplondish men wol likne hem self to gentil men, and fondeth with grete bisynesse for to speke Frensche, for to be the more ytold of' (Trevisa's 'Higden.' 1385). Yet during these 300 years it failed to produce any perceptible effect on the English tongue; none at all, either then or afterwards, on its *structure*, every French word introduced conforming itself ultimately to the English standard: *complainen, compell-ed, apayr-inge* (*disparaging*); this is the testimon-*inge* of Ion. Such forms as cry-*and*, ples-*and*, resound-*and*, inclin-*and*, are not the French part. in *ant*, criant, etc., but the true A.S. participle in -*ende*, -*ande*, -*and*, applied to these French words by analogy with the contemporary forms: see-*and*, mak-*and*, lik-*and*, talk-*and*. Whenever a French participle was retained it lost its participial force and became simply an adjective.

We say 'an *abundant* harvest,' but 'abound-*ing* in fruit,' forming the active participle regularly on the borrowed root.

So little did French affect the vocabulary, that we were able in the last section to classify all the French terms up to that period adopted. Now that it disappears, is ignored and forgotten, it leaves such a deep and lasting impression on the vocabulary, that English from this time ceases to be what it had hitherto remained, a purely Teutonic tongue, and becomes thoroughly Latinized. During the latter half of the fourteenth century such a vast amount of Normanisms was introduced, that all further attempt at classification becomes quite impossible. 'The first great augmentation by foreign words of our Saxon vocabulary was a consequence, although not an immediate one, of the battle of Hastings, and of the Norman domination which Duke William's victory established in our land. . . . The actual interpenetration of our A.S. with any large amount of French words did not find place till very considerably later than this event; however, it was a consequence of it. Some French words we find very soon after; but in the main the two streams of language continue for a long while separate and apart, even as the two nations remained aloof, a conquering and a conquered, and neither forgetting the fact.'—'English, Past and Present.'

HOW ACCOUNTED FOR.

73. Indeed the blending of the two idioms, which now took place, must be looked upon as a result of the fusion of the two races. So long as Saxon continued to be spoken by the peasantry alone, it necessarily remained free from all foreign influence. There was no reason to induce them to substitute terms borrowed from the language of their hated rulers, for those of their own homely speech. But when English began to be spoken universally by all classes, and especially to be employed for literary purposes by the

Anglo-Normans, the case was very different. These writers were still, at least, as familiar with the French as with their newly adopted language, while they were wholly ignorant of A.S., consequently when the English they were acquainted with failed to supply proper terms for abstract, scientific, and refined notions, they were compelled to fall back on the Norman, and introduce such words borrowed from that language freely into their writings. It was, therefore, the adoption of English in literature by the Anglo-Norman portion of the population, that chiefly occasioned the great influx of French words which now took place. To the same circumstance is also to be attributed the universal practice of drawing on foreign sources, adopted by all subsequent writers in the formation of such new terms as they required. They could take them only from those languages they were acquainted with; and as A.S. continued ever after to be neglected and forgotten, and French, after the present age, to be ignored, they naturally had recourse later on to the classic tongues for their supplies.

This view will be confirmed by reference to the relative position maintained for the last 700 years by the English and Irish languages in Ireland. The latter has ceased to be cultivated, has become corrupt and considerably modified in its structure, but it has remained throughout untainted by any great mixture of English, still bearing the same relation to it that Saxon did to the Norman for the first 300 years after the Conquest. This relation ceased in England, and was kept up in Ireland, because in the former country the native element ultimately prevailed, while in the latter it has hitherto failed to do so. The Anglo-Irish, therefore, continuing to look upon the natives as a conquered race, never adopted their language in literature, as the Anglo-Normans did the English. But let us suppose the case of Ireland recovering its freedom, say during the reign of Elizabeth, as the Anglo-Normans were cut off from the Continent during the reign of John. The two races would have necessarily blended in the course of a few generations, the term 'Wilde Irish' would have ceased to be used as a reproach, as did in England the Norman expression 'do you take me for an Englishman?' and for a certainty the language of the masses would have prevailed, and been recognised as the national speech of all classes. But, as an inevitable consequence, when it came to be employed in literature by the Anglo-Irish, it would have been flooded with Anglicisms of every kind, resulting in a language bearing the same relation to the Old Irish as the English now does to A.S. : *structure* Celtic, *Vocabulary* Anglo-Irish, in one case ; *structure* A.S., *Vocabulary* Anglo-Norman in the other.

SPECIMENS—TWO RIVAL SCHOOLS OF LITERATURE, THE NORMAN AND SAXON.

74. Did any doubt remain that the first great inroad of Normanisms was occasioned by writers whose original language was French, and who continued still to live in a French atmosphere, at the same time that they spoke and wrote in English, it would be removed by a glance at the literature of this period. A great deal, both in prose and verse, was composed, especially between the years 1350 and 1400. The authors of the 'Vision concerning Piers the Plowman' and of the 'Creed'—Lawrence Minot, Trevisa, Wickliff, Mandeville, Barbour, Chaucer, and Gower—were all contemporary or nearly so, and a comparison of their works would almost seem to imply that the literary world at the time was divided between two factions, the *Saxon* and the *Norman.* Thus some of these writers introduce foreign metrical systems and a fresh accession of Norman terms, while others endeavour to revive the alliterative poetry of gone-by times, and are more sparing in their use of French words. Robert or William Langland, or whoever is the author of the 'Vision,' may be taken as the best representative of the *Saxon*, Chaucer of the *Norman* school.

At page 13 of the preface to his edition of the 'Saxon Chronicle,' Thorpe remarks: 'From this period [1150] may be dated the break-up of the "old English undefiled." The evil was for some time partial in its influence: its focus was the Norman Court; the Saxon, at least its vocabulary, long kept its ground in the country.; as an example of this may be compared the courtly jargon of Chaucer with the rugged, downright Saxon of "Piers Ploughman."' Here there is of course a good deal of exaggeration, because Mr. Skeat has shown that in point of fact the proportion of French in the 'Vision' (twelve per cent.) is as great as in the 'Canterbury Tales;' nor is it fair to speak of the polished idiom and perfect style of Chaucer as a 'courtly jargon.' Still it is true that his compositions are largely based on foreign models, as we shall presently see, while the author of the 'Vision,' writing solely for the people, rejects rhyme and adheres to the alliterative system peculiar to early English literature.

The other writers of the period lie between these extremes, some inclining one way, some another, according to their Saxon or Norman tendencies. Thus Wickliff, writing in a spirit of antagonism to the Court, the Aristocracy, and the Church, is considerably less affected by Normanisms than Mandeville, who translates his own work out of Latin into French, and 'azen out of Frensche into Englyssch, that every man of my nacioun may undirstonde it.'

The few specimens we have room for will help to illustrate this view of the twofold tendency at work, as well as of the grammatical peculiarities of the Middle English Period.

PIERS PLOUGHMAN'S VISION AND CREED.

75. William Langland's 'Visio Willielmi de Petro Ploughman,' or 'Vision concerning Piers the Plowman,' begun about 1362, is a satirical allegory, somewhat resembling Bunyan's 'Pilgrim's Progress' in its aim, but in verse. It consists of 14,696 short lines distributed into two sections, each containing a series of distinct visions, though the arrangement, contents, and length of the poem differ greatly in the various texts still extant. The author wrote avowedly for the people, and decidedly represents a Saxon school of literature, although not so much in his language as in his poetic system. Rhyme was a Norman innovation; he rejects it, and adheres, as stated, to the A.S. *alliterative* measure already explained. His work is one of the most perfect alliterative poems extant, and, except the 'Creed,' is the last in which alliteration is practised systematically in the South of England.* The rhythm is rather *accentual* than syllabic, the lines being divided into couplets, with *two accented* syllables in the first, and *one* in the second, beginning with the same letter. But in MSS. of this date the couplet is usually run into one long line, the pause being marked by a dot or other orthographic expedient. Thus in the Laud MS. 581, mostly followed by Skeat in his edition (Clarendon Press, 1869), the poem opens thus:

In a sómer séson . whan sóft was the sónnë,
I shópe me in shróudes . as I a shépe (¹) wérë,
In hábite as an hérmite . vnhóly of wórkës,
Went wýde in þis wórld . wóndres to hérë.
Ac on a Máy mórnynge . on Málverne húllës,
Me byfél a férly (²) . of fáiry me thóuȝtë ;
I was wéry forwándred (³) . and wént me to réstë
Vnder a bróde bánke . bi a bórnës sídë,
And ás I láy and léned . and lóked in þe wáteres,
I slómbred in a slépyng . it swéyned so méryë (⁴).
Thanne gan I to meten (⁵) . a merueilouse sweune (⁶),
That I was in a wildernesse . wist I never where ;
As I behelde in-to þe est . an (⁷) hiegh to þe sonne,
I seigh (⁸) a toure on a toft . trielich ymaked ;
A depe dale binethe . a dongeon þere- Inne.
With depe dyches & derke . and dredful of sight.

* 'In the North and West of England alliteration was employed as late as the end of the fifteenth century.'—*Morris's Chaucer: Introduction*, p. 43.

The first portion of this passage is accented, according to Skeat's reading, for the purpose of showing the alliteration and rhythm. The last few lines are left as they stand in the text, and will serve as an exercise for the student. The few obsolete and obscure words requiring explanation are :—

(¹) *Shepe* = shepherd, which reading occurs in some MSS. ; (²) *ferly* = wonder ; (³) *wery forwandred* = worn out with wandering ; (⁴) *merye* = pleasantly ; (⁵) *to meten* = to dream ; (⁶) *sweune* = a dream ; (⁷) *an hiegh* = on high ; (⁸) *seigh* = saw.

With regard to the letter þ occurring in this text, and which still lingers on, occasionally into the next century, Morris remarks that some 'scribes muddle them up in every manner possible, and even turn þ into *y* ; hence the well-known "ye," i.e. þe, for *the*.' (Chaucer, xlix.) But as we have seen that this 'muddle' existed from the beginning, it is to be hoped that uniformity may yet be brought about by the adoption of some such plan as that of Grein, who restricts þ to the beginning and ð to the middle and end of words : 'indem ich hier consequent þ für den Anlaut und ð für den In- und Auslaut durchgeführt habe.' (Bibliothek der A.S. Poesie, I. iv.)

For further information on this most interesting poem see Skeat's various publications, including an excellent paper on the subject contributed by him to Hazlitt's edition of Warton, II. 244.

'Piers Ploughman's Creed,' which should not be confounded with the 'Vision,' is a short satirical poem of 1,697 lines, written by an unknown hand, in imitation of the foregoing, and though considerably more recent (about 1400), is quite as antique in style and structure. Its retention of forms, already partly rejected by Chaucer and his school, shows that great efforts were made to preserve all the inflexions of the last period by the opposite party : wicked folk *betraieth*, and *begileth hem* of *her* good ; and gif *thei* couthen *her* other on Christ leveden ; but the foles *foundeden* hemself; thei *precheth* and *prechen*, *lurketh* and *lurken*; seyne that *her sustren thei ben* that *sogurneth* aboute ; we *sheweth* and we *haven here* made ; we *buildeth*.

CHAUCER—HIS POETIC SYSTEM, GRAMMAR, AND VOCABULARY.

76. But all to no purpose. These compositions could not pretend to compete with the masterpieces of the great father of English poetry, which became universally popular with both parties, and caused his school ultimately to prevail. Chaucer (*d* 1400) was a most voluminous writer; the poetic portion of his great work, the 'Canterbury Tales,' though unfinished, consisting alone of over 17,000 lines; the 'Romaunt of the Rose' (if by him) of nearly 8,000, etc. He is foreign in his poetic system even more than in his vocabulary, having introduced the Italian endecasillabo, which became, reduced by a syllable, the English heroic measure: syllabic and rhyming, as opposed to the old system, *alliterative* and *accentual*, *accent* being, however, equally and alone *essential* to both. The opening of the 'Canterbury Tales,' as accented by Morris, who chiefly follows the Harl. MSS. 7334, will illustrate his grammar, vocabulary, and metre :—

(1) Whan thát *Aprílle* with his schówrës swóotë
(2) The dróught of *Márche* hath *pérced* tó the róotë,
(3) And báthëd évery *véyne* in swich *licoúr*,
(4) Of which *vertúe engéndrëd* is the *floúr*;
(5) Whan *Zéphirús* eëk with his swétë breéthë
(6) *Enspíred* háth in évery hólte and heéthë
(7) The *téndre* cróppës, ánd the yónge sónnë
(8) Hath in the Rám his hálfë *coúrs* i-rónnë,
(9) And smálë fówlës mákën *mélodíe*,
(10) That slépën ál the níght with ópen éyë,
(11) So príketh hém *natúre* in hére *corágës*:—
(12) Thanne lóngën fólk to gón on *pílgrimágës*,
(13) And *pálmërs* fór to seékën *straúnge* stróndës
(14) To férnë hálwës, koúthe in sóndry lóndës

Here it is scarcely necessary to observe that *es* plur. *en*, inf. and plur. pres. *ed* past, final *e* generally, except when elided by a following vowel, should be pronounced as distinct syllables, thus : *schowr-ës* (in l. 1), *perc-ëd* (in 2), *mak-ën* (in 9). Read so, all the verses except (3) and (4), are really endecasyllabic, the last syllable being always unaccented : *mélodí-e* (in 9), *coríg-es* (in 11), *pílgrimág-es* (in 12). Verse (4) consisting of ten syllables strictly (endecasillabo tronco), represents the metre afterwards universally adopted.

All the words in *Italics* in this passage are foreign, and represent not more than the average proportion to be found in the writings of Chaucer. There may be some exaggeration in attributing the great influx of Norman words to him, but there can be no doubt that the fact of his having been the greatest genius of the age, gave, perhaps, undue weight to the Norman school, to which he belonged, and that his influence introduced the practice of borrowing words indiscriminately from foreign tongues. He himself has appropriated a vast number, which have not been retained; and this is true of all his followers. Thus *mel* = honey, *roy* = king, *misericorde* = mercy, *creansur* = creditor, *bainc* = bath, *esperance* = hope, and others pointed out by Trench ('English, Past and Present'). At the same time there is a strange mixture of extreme French and Saxon both in him and in his great admirer, Spenser, which shows that it is writers of the first order who principally enrich and expand the language they employ as the means of giving expression to their boundless thought and imagination. They draw largely upon every available source, for they, more than any others, feel how true it is that more ideas pass through the busy brain of man than all language can supply equivalent terms for.

As a further exercise in the reading of Chaucer, the continuation of the prologue, as far as line 42, is here subjoined, from the Cambridge MS. Gg. 4.27, the gap from line 28 to

Specimens—Chaucer.

36 being supplied from the Harl. MS. 1758, as in F. J. Furnivall's edition, London, 1868.

(¹⁵) And specialy from euerie schires ende
Of Englond to Caunterburye thei wende
The holy blisfull martyr for to seke
That hem hath holpen whan þat) ei were seke.
Byfell that in that sesoun on a daye
In Suthwerk at the Thabard as I laye
Redy to wenden on my pilgrymage
To Caunterbury with full deuoute corage.
At night was come in to þat hostelrye
Well nyne and twenty in a companye
Of sondry folk by auenture falle
In felschip and pilgrymes were þei alle
That towarde Cauntirbury wolde ryde.
[The chambres and the stables weren wyde [Harl. 1758
And well were esid at the beste,
And schortly whan the sonne was to reste
So had I spoken with hem euerychon
That I was of here felaschip anon,
And made forward erly for to ryse
To take oure way there as I you deuyse ;
But natheles while I haue tyme and space
Or that I ferþer in this tale pace]
Me thynketh it a-cordaunt to reson
To telle you all the conclusyoun
Of eche of hem as it semyth me
And whyche þei were and of what degre,
And eke in what aray þat they were inne
And at a knyght þere þanne wele I ferst begynne.

This extract should be read over and over again, in the way already explained, until the reader has acquired perfect ease, and begins to feel the truth of Russell Lowell's remark: 'When I remember Chaucer's malediction upon his scrivener, and consider that by far the larger proportion of his verses (allowing always for change of pronunciation) are perfectly accordant with our present accentual system, I CANNOT BELIEVE THAT HE EVER WROTE AN IMPERFECT LINE.'

SPECIMENS OF PROSE—MANDEVILLE, TREVISA.

77. During the Early English Period not much *prose* that can be called literature was written. While a language is shifting and in a rapid state of transition, it may be very convenient for the poet, by supplying him with a multiplicity of forms, old and new, to suit the exigencies of the metre; but its unsettled state must be felt to be an incumbrance and exceedingly perplexing wherever precision is an object. Hence the earliest compositions amongst all nations are poetic, and none other are possible until the language has acquired a certain consistency. English has now reached this state, consequently prose works become frequent enough. Among the most important and earliest in the language are 'Sir John Mandeville's Travels.' His style, though he is somewhat anterior to Chaucer (died in Liége, 1371), is exceedingly flowing, so much so that it is evident a good deal of prose was written about the same time. In the following passage from the introduction he gives an account of himself and of his work:—

'And for als moche as it is long tyme *passed* that ther was no *generalle passage* ne *vyage* over the sea, and many men *desiren* for to heer speke of the Holy Lond, and han therof gret *solace* and *comfort*, I, John Maundeville, knight, alle be it I be not worthi, that was born in Englond, in the town of St. Albones, *passede* the sea in the yeer of our Lord J. C. 1322, in the day of St. Michelle, and hidre to have ben longetyme over the see and have seyn and gon thorghe manye *diverse* londes, and many *provynces*, and kingdomes, and *iles*, and have *passed* thorghout Turkye, Tartarye, Percie, Ermonie (Armenia). . . . And ye shulle understonde that I have put this boke out of Latyn into Frensch, and *translated* it aȝen out o fFrensche into Englyssch, that every man of my *nacioun* may undirstonde it.' The fourteen words in *Italics* are Norman.

Other prose writers were Chaucer, Trevisa, and Wickliff. Trevisa, a canon of Westbury, in Wilts, finished, in the year 1387, a complete version of the Old and New Testament, the subsequent loss or disappearance of which has occasioned the erroneous impression that Wickliff's (1383) was the only complete translation that preceded the Reformation. Caxton knew of its existence, and mentions it a hundred years after, in the preface to his edition of Trevisa's 'Polychronicon.' The following extract from the latter work alludes to the great diversity in the *spoken* language during the fourteenth century:—

'Hit semeth a grete wonder that Englyssmen have so grete dyversytie on their owin langage in sowne (sound) and in spekyn of it, which is all in one ilonde. . . . Some use straunge, wlaffing, chytrying, harring, garryng, and grysbytyng. The language of the Northumbres, and specyally at Yorke, is so sharpe, slytting, frotyng, and unshape, that we sothern men maye *unneth* * understande that langage.'

In the next passage he informs us that English was substituted for French in schools, as a medium of instruction, about the year 1385:—

'This maner was myche yused to fore the first moreyn (murrain), and is siththe (since) some dele ychaungide; for John Cornwaile, a maistre of grammer, chaungide the lore in grammer scole, and construction of Frensch into Englisch, and Richard Pencriche lerned that maner teching of him, and other men of Pencriche. So that now, the zere of our Lord *a thousand, thre hundred, foure score and fyve*, of the seconde King Rychard, after the Conquest nyne, in alle the gramer scoles of Englond children leveth Frensch, and construeth and lerneth an Englisch, and haveth thereby avauntage in oon side and desavauntage in another.'

* With difficulty.

BARBOUR—LOWLAND DIALECT.

78. The greatest poet of the age, next to Chaucer, was a Scotchman, his contemporary, John Barbour, Archdeacon of Aberdeen (1320—1395). He is the author of the 'Bruce,' a poem of about 12,500 lines, comprising the history of Scotland between the years 1286 and 1330. It is generally assumed that he wrote in the language at the time spoken in the Lowlands; yet the subjoined passage from the opening of the fifth book will suffice to show that. allowing for the northern pronunciation and certain peculiarities of orthography, it is very nearly, if not quite, as intelligible as Chaucer. It begins with a description of Spring, which may be compared with the beginning of the 'Canterbury Tales,' as above quoted:—

> This wes in were (spring) quhen vynter tyde
> Vith his blastis, hydwise to byde,
> Wes ourdriffin : and byrdis smale,
> As thristill and the nychtingale,
> Begouth (begin) rycht meraly to syng,
> And for to mak in thair synging
> Syndry notis, and soundis sere,
> And melody plesande to here.
> And the treis begouth to ma (make)
> Burgeonys (buds) and brycht blwmys alsua,
> To vyn the heling of thar he[v]de,
> That vikkit vyntir had thame revede ;
> And all grewis begouth to spryng.
> In-to that tyme the nobill king,
> Vith his flot and a few menȝe,
> Thre hundir I trow thai mycht weill be,
> [Wes] to the se, furth of Arañe,
> A litill forrow the evyn gañe.
> Thai rowit fast with all thar mycht,
> Till that apon thame fell the nycht,
> That It wox myrky on gret maner,
> Swa that thai wist nocht quhar thai wer.

> For thai na nedill (needle) had na stane,
> But rowit alwayis in-till añe,
> Stemmend alwayis apon the fyre,
> That thai saw byrnand licht and schire !
> It wes bot auentur that thame led :
> And thai in schort tym swa thame sped,
> That at the fyre arivit thai,
> And went to land but mair delay.
>
> (The Cam. MS.* G. 23, ed. Skeat, 1870, I. p. 105.)

Barbour never supposes that he is writing in any other language than *English*. He and his successors, Dunbar and Sydney, never call it by any other name, *Scotch* then and later on still implying the Gaelic or Irish Keltic of the Highlands. More than a hundred years after Barbour, Gawin Douglas (1496—1550), Bishop of Dunkeld, translated the 'Æneid.' He also used the language current in the Lowlands in his time; but that it has already diverged considerably from the southern standard will be evident from the following passage (b. vii. 563, etc.—'Est locus, Italiæ in medio sub montibus altis,' etc.) :—

> 'Amyddis Itale, under the hillis law,
> Thare standis ane famous stede wele beknaw,
> That for his brute is namyt in mony land,
> The vale Amsanctus hate, on ather hand
> Quham the sydis of ane thik wod of tre,
> Closis all derne with skuggy bewis hie ;
> Ane routand burn amydwart thereof rynnis,
> Rumland and soundand on the craggy quhynnis.'

This is more decidedly Scotch, in the modern sense of the word, than is the passage just quoted from Barbour. Two questions, therefore, present themselves: first, how comes a language to be spoken in the Lowlands, during the fourteenth century, which may fairly be called English, and, secondly, how does it happen that this language develops, during the next and succeeding centuries, into what is now

---

* The work was written about 1375, but this MS., which is by far the best, dates only from the year 1487.

called Scotch? The earliest inhabitants of the Lowlands we are acquainted with were the Picts. To these some have traced the Saxon spoken in the country from time immemorial. But the Picts, like all the other primitive inhabitants of the island, were almost certainly Kelts; and even if we suppose them Teutonic, we cannot conceive the corruption of their original Germanic speech resulting in the fourteenth century in a language *identical* with the English corruption of A.S. The *same* language, Latin, has been differently corrupted in Italy, France, Wallachia.

Others have derived the Lowland English from the Scandinavian settlers, who for thirty years, in the eleventh century, maintained a regular kingdom in the East of Scotland. But a *Norse* language never could become an A.S. dialect. The simple explanation is conveyed in the statement that the *Angles* peopled Britain from the Thames to the Clyde. The Northumbrian kingdom ruled the Lothians, and kept the Anglian population united in one nation. At the Conquest, Angles and Saxons poured into Scotland to escape the sword of the invaders. Constant intercourse was maintained between them and those of England throughout the Norman rule, which caused the language of the two countries, originally one, to continue identical, even through a stage of transition (Broken Saxon and Early English Periods), resulting in the Middle English of the fourteenth century, common to both.

But a hundred years later they are no longer the same; one is now *English*, the other *Scotch*. Of the two, this seems the greater difficulty; it has, in fact, occasioned the first, of origin, which we have endeavoured to remove. It may be stated thus: Barbour (fourteenth century) is more English than Douglas (sixteenth), Douglas than portions of Burns (eighteenth). One thing is clear: the history of the growth of the Lowland language begins where that of the English properly ceases (1450, or thereabouts), and the explanation seems to be in its characteristic name of *broad*.

Any difference* which may have existed from the beginning between the Angle or northern, and the Saxon or southern speech, would be more observable in Scotland than elsewhere. The chief difference was one more of *pronunciation* than of *idiom*. The northern, as opposed to the southern dialect, is always represented as characterized by *a broad, drawling* utterance, and a consequent preference for the open vowels *o*, *a*, instead of *e*, *i*. This has been attributed to *Scandinavian* influence. The *Angles* brought the germs of it from the continent, for they came from countries bordering on the *Scandinavian* frontier. It was further developed in the North of England by the Danish settlers in the tenth and eleventh centuries, and still more so in Scotland, by the Norse occupiers of the eastern coast in the eleventh century. The tendency would be checked by an intimate union with the south. Accordingly, it is not very perceptible in literature, so long as that union was maintained; and had Edward II. triumphed at Bannockburn, it would have ultimately disappeared. But if left to itself, and freed from foreign influence, it would work itself out to its legitimate consequences in accordance with a law inherent in all speech. After the war of independence, the two nations were completely isolated, the interests of Scotland inclining it to keep up a close connection with France. Hence the Scottish dialect now began to diverge from the English standard, and it fell off so rapidly that, had the crown of Scotland continued disunited from that of England, it would, in course of time,

---

* Such differences are plainly marked in the Lindisfarne and Rushworth MSS. of the N.T. (§ 28) and in the Lowland poem of 'Lancelot of the Laik,' written probably before 1500, and edited by Skeat for the E. E. T. Soc., 1865. Here we already find *ony*, *mony*, *fecht*, *lap* (past tense of leap), *hard* = heard, *ee* = eye, *tane* = taken, *our* = *ou'er* = over, *low* = love, past tenses in *it* : *closit*, *armyt*, *behovit* ; final *t* and *d* dropped, as in *correk'*, *rown'*, besides many other features of the Scotch dialect, as explained in Lumby's Specimens of '*Louthiane Inglis*.'

have been moulded into a distinct national language. But the accession of James VI. to the throne of England, together with the very great influence of the southern literature before that event, again interfered, and prevented it from assuming more than a peculiar provincial form. Knox, living for many years in England, wrote in English, and others, like Buchanan, feeling that the national speech was becoming every day more of a *patois*, composed in Latin. Thus the independent literature, created and partially developed by the successors of Barbour, Wyntoun, Blind Harry, Lyndsay, Dunbar, Douglas, and others, was not sustained. The 'Complaynt of Scotland,' by an unknown hand, in 1548, was amongst the first and almost the last original prose work in the Lowland language. Verse, from incidental causes, still struggled on, into the eighteenth century; but the general *spread of English* education will prevent Burns from having any successor, and will, perhaps, in a short time cause all dialectical variety to disappear even from the spoken language.

QUESTIONS.

60. What is the extent of the Middle English period? When does it properly cease?

61. Chaucer says: 'Methoughten,' and 'methought;' explain from this the essential difference between the structure of Middle and Early English.

62. When may final *e* in Middle English constitute a syllable? Is Chaucer's metre *syllabic* or only *accentual*?

63. When did final *e French* cease to be pronounced? How were French words gradually conformed to the genius of the English language?

64. What old grammatical endings does final *e* represent? Final *e* adverbial explains the modern use of what appears to be the *adjective* for the adverb?

65. Difference between *possessive* case and *plural* Middle and Modern?

66. Two forms of the infinitive? and of the past part.?

67. How did *lov-eth* come to be pl. in Early, and sing. in Middle

E. ? What is the Middle E. pl. present tense? Why is the pl. *we love*, the same as first sing. I love, in Modern E. ?

68. The past tense had two forms? What was the second pers. imperative?

69. Why is *could*, from *can*, written with an *l?* Original force of *shall* and *will?* It explains their present apparently inconsistent use?

70. In what modern idioms do we find traces of the *true infinitive?* Is '*I can love*' a *mood?*

71. What decree was issued in the reign of Edward III. affecting the language? When did French and Latin cease to be employed in literature?

72. When was English first seriously affected by Normanisms? Was it so affected in its structure?

73. Account for the late influx of French words. To what class of the population do you attribute it?

74. How is this view strengthened by the state of the literature during this period?

75. Give an account of 'Piers Ploughman's Vision,' its language and poetic system, as opposed to those of Chaucer.

76. Scan the Chaucerian couplet:

> And smalle foules maken melodie,
> That slepen al the night with open eye.

Also, the line

> And palmers for to seeken straunge strondes.

77. Who were the principal prose writers of this period? Why is prose generally subsequent to verse? Was Wickliff's the only complete version of Scripture that was now made? Was the spoken language uniform at this time? When was English substituted for French in schools?

78. What is the origin of the Scottish dialect? Account for its identity with English in the fourteenth century, and for its subsequent divergence.

SECTION VI.

MODERN ENGLISH PERIOD (1450).

GRAMMAR—ITS ANALYTIC CHARACTER—CONTRAST—VOCABULARY—LOSS AND GAIN—STYLE—PRESENT POSITION—FUTURE PROSPECTS—CONCLUSION.

MODERN ENGLISH PERIOD—ITS EXTENT.

79. The middle English period is usually protracted to the beginning of the sixteenth century, the 'History of Richard III.,' by Sir Thomas More (1483-1535), being considered 'the first example of good English language, pure and perspicuous, well chosen, without vulgarisms or pedantry'—*Hallam.* Here he is evidently speaking of the style rather than of the structure of the language, for, elsewhere, he observes: 'In following the line of our writers, both in verse and prose, we find the old, obsolete English to have gone out of use about the accession of Edward IV. (1461). . . . In the Paston Letters, in Harding, the metrical chronicler, or in Sir John Fortescue's Discourse on the Difference between an Absolute and a Limited Monarchy, he finds scarce any difficulty; antiquated words and forms of termination frequently occur; but *he is hardly sensible* that he reads these books much less fluently than those of modern times'—*Lit. of Europe.* The following extract, in the original spelling, from the work of Fortescue here cited, will convince us that the only difference between the language he uses and the present, is one of form, and not of structure, orthographical rather than grammatical, both being the same in all essentials. Fortescue, Chief Justice of the King's Bench under Henry VI., flourished between the years 1430 and 1470. Ours is an account of the essential changes the language has undergone from time to time. It must, therefore, close, when those are complete, about 1450 'It is cowardise and lack of hartes and corage, that kepith the Frenchmen from rysing, and not povertye; which corage no Frenche man hath like to the English man. It hath ben often seen in Englond that 3 or 4 thefes, for povertie, hath sett upon 7 or 8 true men, and robbyd them al. But it hath not ben seen in Fraunce that 7 or 8 thefes have ben hardy to robbe 3 or 4 true men. Wherefore it is right seld (*seldom*) that French men be hangyd for robberye, for that they have no hertys to do so terryble an acte. There be therfor mo men hangyd in Englond, in a yere, for robberye and manslaughter, than ther be hangid in Fraunce for such cause of crime in 7 yers.' The little importance that can be attached to the spelling even of inflexional forms is shown by the double form of the past of *hang* in this passage: *hangyd, hangid*; and of the pl. ending: *hartes* and *hertis*. No one can read the whole passage without feeling quite satisfied that the *final e* of the previous stage has already disappeared as a distinct syllable. This single change was sufficient to impart a new and modern air to the language.

FIRST MODERN ENGLISH WRITERS—LYDGATE— JAMES I.—SCOTCH AND BALLAD POETRY.

80. The only English poet, at all worthy of the name, that connects Chaucer (1328-1400) with the first great modern English poet, Thomas Howard, Earl of Surrey (1516-1547), is John Lydgate, a monk of Bury, who flourished about 1430. He therefore belongs, in point of time, rather to the close of the last period, notwithstanding which, and although he formed his style on the school of Chaucer, yet his language is as modern as that of Fortescue. In the appended extract from his 'Destruction of Troy,' it will be seen that he retains or rejects the *final e* syllabic according to the requirements of the metre :

> 'Where from my horse I did alight as fast
> And on the bow aloft his *reinè* cast.
> So faint and mate of weariness I was,
> That I me laid adown upon the grass,
> Upon a *brinkè* shortly for to tell,
> Beside the river of a crystal well :
> And the water, as I *rehersè* can,
> Like *quickè* silver in his streams y-ran,
> Of which the gravel and the brightè stone,
> As any gold, against the sun y-shone.'

This is surely modern English, almost more so than the language of the 'Faerie Queen,' and quite as much as some of Thomson :

> 'But these I *passen* by, with nameless numbers moe.'
> 'And much they moralized as thus *yfere they yode.*'
> 'Withouten that wold come a heavier bale,' etc.
>
> *Castle of Indolence.*

Yfere they yode=together they went, is Broken Saxon for A.S. *geferan hí eódon.*

An earlier and a greater poet than Lydgate was King James I. of Scotland, whose language must be considered rather English than Scotch, slightly tinctured, however, with the peculiarities of that dialect, which were now beginning to develop themselves. He was taken prisoner in his youth by Henry IV., and detained in England for nineteen years, between 1405 and 1424. During this period he composed the only poem that can be safely ascribed to him, 'The King's Quhair,' or Book, in which he describes the romantic attachment he formed for the daughter of the Earl of Somerset, whom he afterwards married. His style is so polished that his retention of the final *e* and full *is=es* pl., alone prevents his being included in the modern period :

' So thick the *boughis* and *leavis* green
　Beshaded all the alleys that there were,
　And mids of every arbour might be seen
　The *sharpé greené sweeté* juniper,
　Growing so fair with branches here and there,
　That as it seeméd to a lyf without,
　The *boughis* spread the arbour all about.
And on the *smallé greené twistis* (twigs) sat
The little *sweeté* nightingale, and sung
So loud and clear, the *hymnis* consecrat
Of *Lovis* use, now soft, now loud among,
That all the gardens and the *wallis* rung
Right of their song.'

The Scottish ballad, 'Edward, Edward,' of uncertain date, but probably a hundred years more recent than this, will serve to illustrate what was said in the last section of the rapid growth of this dialect, at the very time English was becoming a settled language :

' Quhy dois zour brand sae drap wi' bluid,
　　　　　　　Edward, Edward?
　Quhy dois zour brand sae drap wi' bluid?
　　　　　And quhy sae sad gang zee, O?
　O, I hae killed my hauke sae guide,
　　　　　　　Mither, mither:
　O, I hae killed my hauk sae guid;
　　　　　And I had nae mair bot hee, O.'

The ballad poetry of the time was chiefly composed in the Northumbrian dialect, the wandering minstrels being generally represented as north countrymen. Peculiarities, therefore, occasionally present themselves, which give it an antique, sometimes a Scotch, air ; but it is still perfectly modern in its structure :—

'Nethar in Ynglonde, Skottlonde, nar France,
　Nor for no man of a woman born,
　But an fortune be my chance,
　　I dare met him *on* man for *on* (one).

Then bespayke a squyar off Northomberlonde,
Ric. Wytharynton was his nam ;
It shall never be told in Sothe-Ynglonde, he says,
To King Henry the Fourth for sham.'

(*Chevy Chase*—reign of Henry IV.).

CAXTON—INTRODUCTION OF PRINTING—SIR THOMAS MORE.

81. Printing was invented about the year 1440, not earlier. Thirty years later, Caxton (1412–1491) translated and published on the Continent Raoul le Fevre's 'Recueil des Histoires de Troyes,' 'whyche said translacion and werke,' says the title, 'was begonne in Brugis in 1468, and ended in the holy cyte of Colen, 19 Sept., 1471.' In 1474, he issued at Westminster the first book printed in England, also a translation from the French : 'The Game and Playe of the Chesse.' In 1482, he published Trevisa's translation of Higden's 'Polychronicon,' continued by himself from 1357 to 1460, and *modernized*: 'I, William Caxton, a simple person, have endeavoured me to writ first over all the said book of "Polychronicon," and somewhat have changed the rude and old English, that is to wit, certain wordes which, in these days, be neither used ne understood'—*Preface.* The concluding passage of this work, with the spelling restored, will illustrate his own style, which is certainly quainter and less polished than that of Fortescue, inclining more to middle than modern English, and participating more of the two than most writers of this period : 'For yf I coude have *founden moe* storyes, I wold have sette in *hit moo;* but the substaunce that I can fynde and knowe, I have shortly sette *hem* in this book, to *thentente* (the intent) that such *thynges* as have ben done *syth* the deth or ende of the sayd boke of *Polycronycon* shold be had in remembraunce, and not putte in oblyvyon ne forgetynge; prayenge all them that shall see this symple werke to pardone me of my symple and rude wrytynge. Ended the second day of

Juyll the xxii yere of the regne of Kynge Edward the Fourth, and of the Incarnacion of oure Lord a thousand four honderd foure score and tweyne. *Fynysshed per Caxton.*' The words in *Italics* are old English forms, but it is clear that in no single instance does final *e* any longer constitute a syllable. He says *foure* and *four*, *moo* and *moe*, *book* and *boke*; also *hem* and *them*, the *old* and *new* forms, with a disregard for precision remarkable in a man whose first duty should have been to aim at giving the language a settled and consistent character, both in its structure and orthography.

That he was in this respect, whatever be the reason, behind his age, will be evident by comparing the foregoing extract with the following of Sir Thomas More, a few years later on (1480–1535) :—

'Richarde, the third sonne, of whom we nowe entreate, was in witte and corage egall with either of them; in bodye and prowesse farre under them bothe, little of stature; ill-fetured of limmes, croke-backed, his left shoulder much higher than his right, hard-favoured of visage. He was malicious, wrathfull, envious, and from afore his birth ever frowarde.' etc. Nor is his poetic language less pure, as may be seen by the opening lines of his Elegy on Queen Elizabeth, wife of Henry VII., who died in 1503 :—

> 'O ye that put your trust and confidence
> In worldly joy and frayle prosperite,
> That so lyve here as ye should never hence,
> Remember death, and loke here uppon me,
> Ensaumple, I thinke, there may no better be.
> Yourself wotte well that in this realme was I
> Your quene but late, and lo now here I lye.'

EFFECTS OF THE ART OF PRINTING ON THE LANGUAGE.

82. From the foregoing specimens we may safely conclude that the language, in its structure and *grammar*, was

VI.—*Modern English Period.*

completely formed within the fifteenth century, and that the history of its *internal vicissitudes* is now at an end. The Middle and Modern periods are dovetailed one into the other by the names of Fortescue and Caxton. Fortescue (1450) is the first writer who can be called modern; Caxton (1480), the last who can be called old. Nor is it a little remarkable that the perfect formation of the English language was coincident with the introduction of the art of printing into the country. Within fifty years from the death of Chaucer (1400), the great bulk of inflexional forms, explained in the last section as peculiar to Middle English, seem to have already disappeared. Since that time no further loss has been sustained. All the grammar, strictly speaking, which the language then possessed, it still retains, any change which is since then observable being only such as all spoken speech must be liable to, referring to matters of style, propriety of idiom and expression, and especially the vocabulary. It is obvious that some cause has been at work to check the tendency to *perfect analysis*. Literature would have always done a great deal, and retarded this result indefinitely. But it did not save the verbal and case-endings of the Chaucerian age, even for a single generation; nor would it in all probability have ultimately preserved the few that seem now finally settled, had its influence not been more than doubled at first by the invention of printing, and subsequently increased tenfold by the general extension of this wonderful art. That literature alone would have been inadequate to transmit them to our times, may be deduced from the fact that all the weight and authority of the name of Shakspeare has failed to prevent from growing more or less obsolete some 2,000 words actually used by him, although his works are more diffused and better known than those of any other writer.

UNSETTLED STATE OF THE ORTHOGRAPHY.

83. The immediate effect of printing was, however, least felt where it might have been most expected, and certainly was most required. It found the orthography in so confused and perplexing a state, that the only standard of spelling seems to have been the individual taste and fancy of the writer, and in that state it allowed it to continue for centuries.* Such a thing as bad spelling in those days was unknown, because every one spelled as he pleased, differing not only from every one else, but from himself. We have just seen Caxton *printing* the same word differently in the same passage and even sentence. Later on, Tyndal published his version of the N. T. (1525), in which he spells the pronoun *it* in no less than eight different ways : *it, itt, yt, ytt, hitt, hit, hyt, hytt*, four or five occurring sometimes in the same page. A passage from *St. Luke* (xvi.) he cites in a subsequent work, 'The Parable of the Wicked Mammon' (1536), but no longer in the same orthography, both varying most ingeniously from that of Cranmer's Bible (1539) and the Geneva N. T. (1557) :—

Tyndal's Bible (1525).	Wicked Mammon (1536).	Cranmer's Bible (1539).	Geneva New Testament (1557).
certayne	certain	certayn	certain
rych	riche	ryche	riche
which	whiche	whych	which
with in	within	wythin	within
moche	muche	moch	muche

* 'I, your gracis humble servant, seeing sik uncertentie in one men's wryting, as if a man wald indyte one letter to tuentie of our best wryters, nae tuæ of the tuentie, without conference, wald agree ; and that thay quhæ might perhapes agree, met rather be custom then knawlege, set my selfe, about a year syne, to seek a remedie for that maladie.' *Of the Orthographie and Congruitie of the Britan Tongue,* be Alexander Hume, Head Master of the Edinburgh High School, dedicated to James I., and edited by H. B. Wheatley, London, 1865.

Tyndal's Bible (1525).	Wicked Mammon (1536).	Cranmer's Bible (1539).	Geneva New Testament (1557).
fyrst	firste	first	fyrst
everlastinge	everlasting	everlastynge	everlasting
bill	byl	byll	—
steward shippe	stewardshypp	stewardshyp	stewardeshyp
stewarde shippe	stewardshypp	stewardeshyppe	stewardshyp
stewardshippe	*stewardship*	*stewardship*	stewardshyp

The last word is curious and instructive. It shows the efforts that were made by the writers to hit upon a satisfactory plan, in some instances resulting in the form finally adopted. It is also evident from these variations that the sound of the word was pretty much what it now is, and that, therefore, the language of the period is, in reality, less different from the present than it sometimes appears to be, disguised in the uncouth garb of clumsy spelling.

No systematic attempt was made at uniformity until the time of Johnson, who observes in his preface that the orthography 'has been to this time unsettled and fortuitous'; and although, since the publication of his great Dictionary, it may be regarded as having assumed a comparatively determined form, yet even now not isolated words, but whole classes, are in a fluctuating state, such as those in *-ick*, *-our*, *-el*, *p*, *-t*, *-ize*, etc. We now write *music, public, logic*, without hesitation; *error, dolor, tumor*, confidently; *honor, favor, endeavor, Savior*, not without some mistrust; *dueling, traveling, reveling*, at a venture; and are fairly perplexed when we come to select between *worshipped* and *worshiped, civilize* and *civilise*. In the last edition of Worcester's Dictionary there is a list of about 1,800 words of 'doubtful or various orthography.'

THREE CAUSES OF IRREGULARITY — CHANGE OF ALPHABET—CHANGE OF PRONUNCIATION—DEFECTIVE ALPHABET.

84. Three causes seem to have coöperated in rendering our present orthographic system the most inconsistent and irregular in the world: (a) *change of alphabet*, (b) *change of pronunciation*, and (c) *radically defective alphabet*.

CHANGE OF ALPHABET.

(a) The A.S. alphabet, laid aside during the Early English Period, consisted of 24, ours of 26 letters; but we gained little by the substitution, having rejected two, þ and ð, which are now badly wanted, and one, æ, not quite superfluous. Of the five additional characters *j, k, q, v, z, three* only, *j, v, z*, are really useful, k=*hard c*, and q=*kw*, being redundant. But the change itself was productive of the greatest possible amount of confusion, as explained in Sec. IV.

CHANGE OF PRONUNCIATION.

(b) This was not a little increased by the change of pronunciation which has been going on from the earliest times, generally without a corresponding change of spelling. The sound changes and the form remains.* Reference to the A.S., and especially to the *living* cognate tongues, proves that *b* in *tomb, dumb, climb*; *l* in *calf, half, walk*; *k* in *knee*,

---

* Since this was written A. J. Ellis's great work on *Early English Pronunciation* has been in progress (1868-75). Yet I see no reason to alter this passage, believing, as I do, that the learned writer's premises are often erroneous, and that consequently many of his conclusions cannot be accepted. His axiom, for instance, that 'the orthography shows the sound,' I hold to be utterly untenable, and is in fact refuted by the very authorities he relies upon. Thus Salesbury, the author of our earliest existing work on pronunciation (1567), speaks of the 'diversitie of pronounciation' of the vowel *e* in his time, 'in certain words, such as "bere," beer or bear; "pere," peer or pear; "hele," heel or heal, and "mele," ground corn or portion.' Yet Mr. Ellis ventures to assert that *e* was always sounded like the *e* of *get*. And so with the long sound of *i* as in *fine*, which he believes to be quite modern, but which I think it would not be difficult to show must have been pre-historic, and common to the whole Teutonic race before it split up into its now clearly marked divisions—High German, Low German, and Norse. Hence it is satisfactory to know that this work has already elicited a vigorous protest in opposition to its conclusions by Mr. R. F. Weymouth in his very able treatise on *Early English Pronunciation*. Asher, 1874.

knock; *gh* in *right, high, through, dough, tough, cough, hiccough*, were not originally mute or irregular as now. The dramatist Lyly (born 1554) seems to have effected a sort of temporary revolution in the language generally, and especially in the pronunciation, by the publication in 1578 of his prose romance of 'Euphues, or the Anatomy of Wit.' The influence of his school, as it is called, of *Euphuism*, was for some time very great, especially at court and with the ladies. Blount, writing in 1632, says that 'our nation are in Lyly's debt for a new English, which he taught them. "Euphues and his England" began first that language: all our ladies were then his scholars; and that beauty in court which could not parley Euphuism . . . that *pure* and *reformed English*,' which he introduced, was as little regarded as those who are now ignorant of French. But Euphuism soon died out, though it may have tended very much to soften the language at the time, and certainly effected a lasting change in the pronunciation of a considerable number of words. Holofernes, the schoolmaster in 'Love's Labour's Lost,' complains bitterly to Sir Nathaniel of a system, seemingly new in his time, but now firmly established: 'I abhor such fanatical fantasms, such insociable and point-devise companions, such *rackers* of *orthography* as to speak *dout* fine, when he should say *doubt*; *det*, when he should pronounce *debt, d, e, b, t*; not *d, e, t*; he clepeth a *calf, caufe*; *half, hauf*; *neighbour*, vocatur *nebour*; *neigh* abbreviated *ne*: this is abhominable (which he would call *abominable*), it insinuateth me of insanie' (Act V. 1); as to attempt to restore the worthy pedant's utterance of these words, would 'insinuate of insanie' any man at the present day.

DEFECTIVE ALPHABET.

(c) Not a less fruitful source of irregularity is the *radically defective* nature of the present alphabet, more sensibly felt now than formerly, because Modern English possesses several vowel and consonantal sounds unknown to the

A.S., and probably occasioned by the introduction of the French element. Thus the sound of *s* in *pleasure, leisure*= French *j*. The consequence is, that the English alphabet is by far the most imperfect and incomplete of all others. It supplies only twenty-three distinct letters for at least forty-four distinct sounds; for *c*=either *k* or *s*, *q*=*kw*, and *x*=ks, must be subtracted from the number twenty-six, as superfluous, leaving twenty-one sounds of the spoken language, without any written representatives.

The vowel sounds are altogether twenty, with five equivalents only, employed in a most arbitrary manner:

a = 5, as in *fat*,[1] *fast*,[2] *aunt*,[3] *far*,[4] *fall*.[5]
e = 2, as in *sell*,[1] *sale*.[2]
i = 3, as in *sin*,[1] *seen*,[2] *sign*.[3]
o = 3, as in *not*,[1] *nor*,[2] *note*.[3]
u = 5, as in *fur*,[1] *tub*,[2] *full*,[3] *fool*,[4] *few*.[5]

Diphthongs. { oi = 1, as in *boy*.
{ ou = 1, as in *bow*.

The distinct consonantal sounds are twenty-four, expressed by eighteen distinct characters and six combinations; and even two of these are redundant; *gh*=g hard, *ph*=f; and one equivocal *th*=þ and ð. The twenty-four consonantal sounds are: b, ch, d, dh=ð=th in *then*, f, g *hard*, h, j, k, l, m, ng, n, p, r, s, sh, t, th=þ=th in *thin*, v, w, y, z, zh=j French, as in *delusion, intrusion, treasure, measure*.

GRAMMAR—NUMBER OF ACTUAL ENDINGS IN MODERN ENGLISH.

85. The difference between the grammar of Middle and Modern English consists in the disappearance from the latter of the inflexions explained as peculiar to the former in the last section (§ 61–67), and should be there studied. Here it has all been pure loss, no gain. The tendency throughout has been to throw off all the existing forms in the language, not to revive old or invent new ones. Any accession, therefore, must have accrued from foreign sources, Norman or Latin. But it cannot be too strongly insisted upon that such a mixture of grammar as this would imply, is a rare phenomenon in any language, and is unknown to the English. The Greeks would not tolerate even a proper name until it put on a Greek appearance, and submitted itself to the laws of their grammar. Hence Jerusalem becomes *Hierosolyma*; Astarte, *Astroarche* (the star-ruler), and the Byzantine writers, at a time when the language was breaking up, always decline and conjugate regularly any terms they appropriate from the Westerns : οἱ καβαλλάριοι -ιων -ιους, *Chevaliers*, τουρνέσειν from τουρνέμεντον.

Accordingly, there is no single accession to English grammar from any foreign quarter. The few forms that still survive are the wreck of the A.S. system, developed in Section II., and, in the following table, may be traced down from it through the different periods here treated. The whole body of actual and possible inflexions is only twenty-five, of which sixteen are fixed and appropriated by the pronouns : *mine, my, me,* etc. The nine moveable forms available for general application are : noun 1, *s* or *'s* ; adj. 2, *er, est* ; verb 6, *est, eth, s, ed, edst, ing* ; three of which, *est, eth, edst,* as well as three of the pronominal forms, *thine, thy, thee,* have already disappeared from the spoken language. If we reflect that such forms as the irregular plur. in *-en,* or by a change of vowel, *oxen, teeth,* etc. ; the gen. in *-r, our, your, their* ; the dat. or acc. in *-m, him, them, whom* ; the strong præterites, *broke, gave* ; the present of *be, am, art, is, are*; the past of *wesan, was, were,* etc., are stationary and incapable of further use, we may conclude that the English language has reached a perfect state of analysis, short of just six noun and verbal endings : *-s* or *-'s,** *-er, est* ; *-s, -ed,** *ing,*

---

* The variations *-es, -t, churches, boxes, clipt, blest,* &c., are mere matters of euphony, just as *s* in reality is pronounced *z* after a flat : land*z*, head*z*, though written lands, heads.

the same number that a single tense of any French, Italian, or Latin verb presents : *-o, -as, -at, -amus, -atis, -ant.* However, in the table account will be taken of the principal existing forms, in order to show that such as they are they must all be referred to the one native source. The plural *s* might occasion some doubt, being apparently derivable from the Norman as well as the Saxon. But it has been shown, in Section III., that the Norman had not even any indirect influence in causing a preference for one Saxon declension rather than for another.

HISTORICAL TABLE OF ENGLISH ACCIDENCE.

86. In each stage of the language there always existed, side by side, double forms, a strong and a weak, the former disappearing at the next stage, and the latter then becoming the strong, with a further softening for the weak, and so on. The A.S. plural of the past tense was both *lufoden* and *lufedon;* in Broken Saxon *lufodon* goes out, *lufedon* becomes the strong, *lufeden* the weak form; in Early English, *lufeden* and *loveden;* in Middle English, *lovédén* and *lovédé;* in Modern English, *lovéd* and *lov'd.* In the table, the strong form of each period has been selected in preference, in order to mark more distinctly the gradations from one to the other. In the modern, however, it was necessary to give the spoken or weak form, the written being deceptive : *have = hav(e).*

HISTORICAL TABLE OF ENGLISH ACCIDENCE.
NOUN.

Anglo-Saxon.	Broken Saxon.	Early English.	Middle English.	Modern English.
cyning	cining	king	king	king
cyninges	cininges	kingis	kinges	king's
cyningas	ciningas	kingis	kinges	kings
cyninga	cingene	kingenen, kingenes	kinges	kings' (Gen. pl.)
			of kinges	of kings
heortan	heorten	heortis	heartes	heart's
bóc	bóc	bok	boke	book
béc	boces	bokis	bokes	books
bóca	boce	bokis	bokes	books'
cycenu	cicene	kiken, kikens	chicken, chickens	chickens
cildru	cildra, childre	childer, N.	childeren	children
brothru	brothre, brothren	brethre, brether, N., bretlren	brotheres, bretheren	brothers, brethren
dohtru	dohtre	dohtren, degter, N., dehtren	doughtren, doughteres	daughters
oxan	oxan	oxen	oxen	oxen
manna	mannes	mennis	mennes	mens' (Gen. pl.)
pennegas	pennyas	pennyes	pans, pens	pennies, pence
ægru	eyre	eyren	egges	eggs
eagan	eyan	eyen	eyghen, cyne	eyne, eyes, een
fan	fon	fone	foen	foes
scon	schon	schoen, schone	shoon	shoes

Historical Table of English Accidence.

ADJECTIVE.

Anglo-Saxon.	Broken Saxon.	Early English.	Middle English.	Modern English.
fægera	fæire	of fayre	of faire	of fair (pl.)
se fægra	þe fæiror	the fayror	the fayrer	the fairer
fægreste	fæireste	fayreste	fayrest	fairest
swiftena	swiftene	of swifte	of swifte	of swift (pl. def.)
swiftra	swiftre	of swifte	of swifte	of swift (pl. indef.)
gelic	iliche	ilich	liké	like, ly
fægerlice	fæierliche	fayrliche	fayrlike	fairly
fægrost	fæierest	fayerest	fayrest	fairest (adv.)
(lytel) læsse	læsse	lasse	lesse	less
(yfel) wyrrest	wirrest	worest	worest	worst
dægwamlic	dægwamlic	deywamlie	dayelie	daily

PRONOUN.

Anglo-Saxon.	Broken Saxon.	Early English.	Middle English.	Modern English.
user	ure	oure	our	our
ge	ge	yhe	ye	ye, you (nom.)
eow, eowic	geow, zuw, ow	yhou, zou, ou	zow, you	you (acc.)
hine (acc.)	hine, hin	hin, him	him	him (dat. and acc.)
hi, hig	hi, hie, heo	hi, hii, þai, þei	þei, þai	they
hira, heora	heore, hire	here, hir, þair	hir, þair, thar	their
heom, him	heom, hem, ham	hem, hom, þam	hem, þam, þem	them
hit, his	hit, his	hit, it, his	hit, it, his	it, its
heo	heo, hi, *scæ**	heo, hi, sco, scho	ho, scho, sche	she
hire	hire, heore, here	here, hire	hire, hir	of her
hwa, hwæt	hwae, hwet	huo, hwo, buet, hwat	hwo, who, wat, what	who, what

* In Sax. Chron. (Stephen) *Morris, Historical Outlines*, p. 270.

VI.—*Modern English Period.*

VERB.

Anglo-Saxon.	Broken Saxon.	Early English.	Middle English.	Modern English.
hæbbe	habbe	hafe	have	I hav(e)
hafast	hafast	hafast	havest, hast	hast
hafað	hafath	hafethth	haveth, hath	has
hafað	hafeð	hafeth	hafeth, haves, haven, han	hav(e) pl.
hæfde	hafde	hedde	hadde	I had
hæfdest	hafdest	heddest	haddest	hadst
hæfdon	hafden	haddlen	hadden, hadde	had, pl.
habban	habben	to hafen	to haven, han	to hav(e)
to habbenne	to habben	}		
hæbbende	habbende	hafande, hafende	havand, having	having
clænsende	clensende	clensande	clensend, clensing	cleansing (participle)
clænsung	clensung	clensynge	clensing	cleansing (noun)
weop*	weop	wop	weped	wept
gehatan†	ihoten	ihote	ihight	hight
cleopode	clupode	clepede	cleped	clept
weorðan	worden	worthen	worthe‡	to be

---

* 'Myne herte *wop* for grete dred{e}.'
A. Davie, A.D. 1312.

This is but one of a number of *strong* preterites displaced by the weak form. Both often exist side by side, *wrought, worked*. The *strong* must ultimately yield in all cases, unless it change its meaning and become an adjective, as here.

† The prefix *ge* seems to be itself a weaker form of the more archaic *gi*, which occurs in the Ruthwell Cross Inscription in the line : miþ strelum *giwundad* = wounded with darts.

‡ The loss of this auxiliary, *worth* = *fieri*, is one of the greatest the language has sustained. For want of it we have no equivalent to the present passive in Latin and other languages. *I am loved* = *amatus sum*, not to

Anglo-Saxon.	Broken Saxon.	Early English.	Middle English.	Modern English.
eom	eam, beom	beo, eam	be, am	am be
eart	earð, beost	bist, erð (?)	bist, eart	art, beest
is	is, beoth	beth, is	bith, bes, is	is
syndon sinden	} sind, beoth	beth, aron	arn, are, beon	are, be
waeron	weoren	wearen	weren	were
wesan	wesen, beon	ben	ben, be	to be
wesende	wesend	beand	beend, being	being
gewesen	ywesen	yben	ben, been	been

EARLY ENGLISH DIALECTS.

(Oliphant's 'Standard English,' p. 63.)

North . . .	We standes singande.
Midland . . .	We standen singende.
South . . .	We standeth singinde.
Modern . . .	We stand singing.

amor. It was still in use throughout the Middle English period : 'My joye is tourned in to strife—that sobre shall I never *worthe*' (*Gower*), and retained long after by the Scotch *in multis saxonizantes*: 'Ever as the battle *worthis* mair cruel' (*Douglas*). It occurs even now in the expression *woe worth*, common in Spenser and later writers: 'wo worth, wo worth ye, my merry men all' (*Ballad of Little Musgrave*); 'woe worth the day' (*W. Scott*); 'wo worth the man' (*Spenser*). Compare also the German werden: ich werde geliebt = amor.

ANOMALOUS FORMS—PLURALS IN EN.

87. Most of these forms actually occur in the writers of the several periods; such as do not, have been formed by analogy. A few seem to require further explanation. *Chick-en* is universally believed to be the old pl. of *chick*, as *ox-en* is of *ox*, the modern *chick-ens* being considered an instance of a double pl., occasioned by ignorance of the original pl. force of *-en* in a certain class of A.S. words: '*Sunt qui dicunt* in singulari "chicken," et in plurali "chickens."' (*Wallis*). Yet here *-en* is not the A.S. pl. *-an* of the def. or simple declension (§ 18), but a diminutive A.S. ending: *cóc*=*cock*, *cycen*=*chicken*, with an irregular pl. *cycenu*. If in Sussex 'they would as soon think of saying "oxens" as "chickens"' (*Trench*), we can only conclude that provincialisms are not always infallible. So also the *-in* of *welkin* from *wolcen*, pl. *wolcenu*, is radical, though generally assumed to be originally pl. *Child-r-en*, on the other hand, from *cild*, pl. *cild-ru*, is an instance of a double pl. which has not been satisfactorily accounted for. The old form is still retained in the Irishism *childer*, proving that the additional *n* was subsequent to the English invasion. The *r* of *breth-r-en* is radical, and the *-en* is pl., not explained by the A.S. *broðor*, pl. *gebroðra*, *broðra*, and *broðru*. The further change of the radical vowel *o* into *e* would imply a Norse affinity: broder, pl. bröder (Swedish). Nor is the *n* of *swine* originally pl.: A.S. *swin*, pl. *swinas*. It is a distinct word from, not a pl. of, *sow*=*sug* and *sugu*. Shakspeare says properly, 'O monstrous beast! how like *a swine* he lies!' By comparing *cow*, *kine*, with *cu*, pl. *cý*, and *man*, *men*, with *man*, pl. *menn* irreg., it will appear that the only real remnant of the A.S. def. declension is *ox*, *ox-en*, from *oxa*, *oxan*.* Another instance would be *een* and

---

* Morris arrives at the same conclusion: 'There were a larger number of these words in the oldest English which formed the plural

eyne for *eyes*, from *eáge*, pl. *eágan*: 'our watry eyne' (*Shaks.*). But it is now obsolete, though retained in Scotch *ee*, *een*, which is said in many respects to be 'Anglica hodierna purior' (*Casaubon*). The two plurals *shoes* and *shoon*, were both found in the irreg. pl. *sceós, scós, gescý*, and *scon, sceón* of *sceó, sco, scoe=shoe*.

THREE DIALECTS—NORTHERN, MIDLAND, SOUTHERN.

88. These and other old English forms not existing in the written A.S., such as *doghten*=A.S. *dóhtra, bishopen*= *bisccopas, treen=treowas, sustren=sweostra*, only prove that the A.S. we are acquainted with represents, after all, but one variety, that of Wessex, whereas in reality the spoken language was at all times split up into a number of dialects, distinguished by certain peculiarities, amongst which may have been a more general pl. in *-en* than is found in the classic language of Alfred. Higden mentions three distinct dialects prevalent in his time (fourteenth century)—the northern, the southern, and the midland or Mercian. 'In the above three-fold Saxon tongue, which has barely survived among a few country people, the men of the east agree more in speech with those of the west, than the northern men with the southern. Hence the Mercians or Midland English, partaking, as it were, the nature of the extremes, understand the neighbouring dialects, the northern and the southern, better than those last understand each other. The whole speech of the Northumbrians, especially in Yorkshire, is so harsh and rude, that we southern men cannot understand it.' It is generally believed that it was the union of the midland and southern which produced the present literary language, just as the northern siding with the Lowland ultimately resulted in the modern Scotch.

in *an*; only *one* is now in common use, oxen = O. E. oxan.'—*Outlines*, p. 95.

These inflexions in *-en*, now obsolete, may therefore be referred to the midland element, and may help to confirm the statement of Sir F. Madden, that 'the dialects of the western, southern, and midland counties contributed together to form the language of the twelfth and thirteenth centuries, and consequently, to lay the foundation of modern English.' But in his 'Standard English,' Oliphant puts in a strong claim for the northern and east midland dialects, and he certainly does show that there is a larger Norse element in English than had been previously suspected. It has been remarked by competent judges that the provincial speech of Berkshire, the native place of Alfred, resembles most the written A.S., while that of Leicestershire and neighbouring counties, which is 'remarkable for its want of tone, has contributed more than any of our other living dialects to the formation of our present standard English.'—' Engl. Rhythms, in Craik's Outlines.'

THE MODERN PRONOUNS—IT AND ITS.

89. In the comparative table all the modern inflexions are accounted for, except the gen. of *it*, *its* for *his*; *th* for *h* in *they*, *them*, *their*; and the *s* in the third pers. sing. pres. indicative for *eth* or *th*, *has* for *haveth*, *hath*. The substitution of *its* for *his* is one of the most singular instances in the language of the importance sometimes attaching to little words and grammatical anomalies. The change is not only modern, but even recent, being still almost unknown in the provincialisms of the south of England. It began about the time of Shakspeare, who uses both forms, but more commonly *his*:

> 'Who can impress the forest, bid the tree
> Unfix *his* earthbound root?' (*Macbeth*).

Bacon writes: 'Opium loses some of *his* poisonous qualities'; Carew: 'This rule admitteth *his* exceptions'; and the Anglican Bible: '*his* shaft and *his* branch, *his* bowls, *his* knops and *his* flowers,' speaking of the candlestick (*Exod.* xxxvii.). *Its*, in fact, never once occurs throughout the whole of that version. But it is met with in the poems forged by Chatterton in the last century, as the productions of a Monk Rowlie, living in the fifteenth:—

'Life and all *its* goods I scorn.'

The famous controversy which they occasioned would have been prevented, and the cheat at once detected, had attention been paid to this single point. The substitution is doubtless an advantage, adding much to the clearness of the language, and was probably occasioned by the necessity of distinguishing between *his* masc. and *his* neut. *His* was considered as more properly the gen. of *he*, and a new gen. was created for *it* by analogy: *it, its*, like *man, man's* (see Sec. V. § 67, *ad finem*).

THE FORMS THEY, THEIR, THEM, MY, THY, &c.

90 The change from *hi, hire*, and *hem* to *they, their, them* goes much further back, traces of it occurring early in the thirteenth century in the northern dialects. The oldest forms are *thei, tha* (usually identified with the plural of the A.S. definite adjective þa); þair, thar, there; þam, þem, &c. In the south the West Saxon forms held their ground much longer, and *'em=hem=them* is still heard in the spoken language. Chaucer uses both forms, but prefers the old, while his northern contemporary, Barbour, almost invariably adopts the modern *thai, thar, thaim* :—

> The King that nycht his wachis set,
> And gert ordayne that THAI mycht et;
> And bad THAIM comford to THAIM tak,
> And at THAR mychtis mery mak.
> *The Bruce*, III., 187-190.

But although the substitution may, to some extent, be due to northern influence, reference to the kindred tongues shows that the A.S. *hi, heora, heom* must themselves be treated as corruptions, perhaps peculiar to the southern or West Saxon dialect. Hence the modern forms may, in this instance, be looked upon as a return to the more primitive ones, which had never died out in the Northumbrian and Scottish dialects:—

Gothic	thai	thaim	thize
Lithuanian	tie	tiemus	—
Slavonian	ti	tiem	—
O. H. German	diê	dêm	dero
Norse	their	theim	theirra
Northumbrian	thai	thaim	thar
Modern English	they	them	their
West Saxon	˙hí	heom	heora

Without going beyond the Slavonic and Teutonic groups, this table clearly shows that the dental is prehistoric. Our modern forms need not, therefore, be derived, with Morris and other recent philologists, from the 'plural of the definite article, O.E. *tha*, probably modified by Scandinavian influence.'—' Historical Outlines,' p. 120.

The necessity, again, of avoiding confusion seems to have occasioned this revival: *heom* softened to *him* was no longer distinguishable from *him* sing.; *heora* to *hira, hire, hir, her* from *her* fem. sing.; *hi* from *he*.

Many of these forms, such as *my, his, their*, etc., are constantly called *possessive pronouns* instead of possessive *cases* of *personal* pronouns. If *I, he, they*, are personal pronouns, they must remain such throughout their inflexions, for a word cannot be one thing in one case and another thing in another, a noun in the sing., an adjective in the pl. Real poss. pronouns partake of the nature of adjectives, agreeing with the *thing possessed:* caput *suum*. These, on the contrary, stand for, and agree with, the possessor: *his, her* head. Of the two, the latter seems the more logical expression, and it will be generally found that the structure of the English is more consistent with sound reason than that of most languages, the peculiar forms they assume depending much upon the national genius. The strong practical turn of the English mind is well illustrated by the present state of English Grammar, in which everything has been rejected which appeared superfluous, and such inflexions alone retained as were absolutely required for the sense. The noun has preserved a pl. ending, the adjective remaining unchanged. It was thought more rational to make the pronoun in all cases agree with the person it stood for, and common sense evidently suggested the present philosophic arrangement of gender, by which English is distinguished from all other European languages. The tendency to analysis may therefore be said to have been guided and influenced by a sort of national instinct, causing it to result in a system unsurpassed for clearness and simplicity.

VERBAL FORMS—PRES. INDIC.—PARTICIPLES.

91. The existence, side by side, from the earliest times, of the two forms for the third pers. pres. indicative, *loveth* and *loves*, is an additional proof that the written language has resulted from the fusion of the different spoken varieties. *Th* seems to be peculiarly southern, from A.S. ð and að; and *lov'th, read'th, zee'th, rain'th*, are still heard in Somerset, where the old southern dialect is best preserved. Dolman, in the sixteenth century, writes :—

> 'So mid the vale, the grayhound seeing stert
> His fearful foe pursu'th, before she fler'th,
> And where she turn'th he turn'th her there to beare,
> The one prey prick'th, the other saefties feare.'

On the other hand, the Northumbrian shows, as we have seen, a preference for *s*, even in the plural. Barbour has *giffis* where Chaucer would say *giveth*, *mayse* for *maketh*, *levys* for *liveth*, and the Scottish ballad of the *Jew's Daughter* begins :—

VI.—*Modern English Period.*

> ' The rain *rins* doun through Mirry-land toune (Milan),
>   Sae *dois* it doune the Pa (the Po):
>   Sae *dois* the lads of Mirry-land toune,
>   Quhan they play at the ba'.'

James I. terminates all his plurals in *s:* he *loves*, we, ye, they *loves;* just as in Early English they said: he *loveth*, we, ye, they *loveth*. The present of *give* in the different periods and dialects shows that the modern form is northern and Scotch rather than southern:—

			Middle E.				
Saxon.	*Early E.*	*South.*	*North.*	*Modern.*	*Kent.*	*Wexford.*	*Scotch.*
gife	gife	give	giffes	giv(e)	yef	gi'	gie
gifst	gifest	givest	giffist	givest	yefst	gi'st	gie'st
gifð	gifeth	giveth	*giffis*	*giv(e)s*	yefth	gi'th*	*gie's*
pl. {gifað / gife}	gifeth	giveth } given }	giffis	giv(e)	yef	gi'th	gie

The forms *hav-and* and *clens-ing*, in the fourth column (p. 140), point out the time when the active part. in *-ende* began to be confounded with the verbal substantive in *-ing* and *-ung*, explained in Sec. IV. § 52. Here it may be observed that this participle, in many grammars, is wrongly called *present* instead of *active*. It properly implies action as opposed to passion, being quite indifferent as to *time:* I *am, was,* and *will be* loving. So also the participle in *-ed* is not *past* rather than present or future: I *am, was, will be* loved; but always passive, even in such phrases as, 'I have written a letter'='I have a letter written.' It is not creditable to English philology that the handful of inflexions surviving in the language are not even yet always properly understood or correctly set forth.

---

* 'He et nou*th* fade t'zey ee'lean vetch eeman' [He that knows what to say, mischief fetch the man]. See, in the first number of the ATLANTIS, an interesting paper by Dr. Russell, President of Maynooth, on this curious old Saxon dialect, surviving until recently in the barony of Forth, county Wexford. He observes, that 'it appears to partake of the vocabulary of each of the three great English provincial groups —the Northumbrian, the Mercian, and the Saxon, but especially of the last. Moreover, judging from the inflexions of the verb, and from the *participial forms*, it seems to me to belong to a period especially requiring illustration.'

RELATIONAL WORDS—THEIR REAL NATURE.

92. Hitherto account has been taken only of the *notional* words, which are alone subject to inflexion. It is obvious that the number of *relational* words must increase in proportion as the inflexions disappear.* Accordingly we find a great variety of them in modern English, employed in a multiplicity of ways not always easy of explanation. Their very right to be considered as words at all has been questioned, on the ground that they do not answer to the strict logical definition of a term : 'vox ideam exprimens.' *At, from, by,* are indeed *voces,* or articulate sounds, but seemingly not *termini,* being meaningless in themselves, and employed only as substitutes for the old case-endings *-an, -um, -ena,* which nobody ever maintained to be terms.* Here it is necessary to distinguish between relational terms *living* and *dead,* between those that still possess an independent existence of their own, and those that are now destitute of any intrinsic value, between, for instance, *do,* used as an auxiliary, and the conjunction *if.* The former present no difficulty, being clearly terms in the strict sense ; the latter, whether explicable or not by reference to A.S., all sound linguists now agree in considering as originally true words, like any other, which, by constant use, have come to lose their primitive force, and to be employed only as particles.† Such a thing as a deliberate invention of a conjunction or preposition, any more than of a case or verb-ending, otherwise void

---

* 'The use of relational words (Formwörter) is increased especially in a language, such as the English, in which the endings become weakened by the mixture of a foreign element. . . . On the other hand the use of relational words itself brings about a weakening of the endings, as, for instance, in the Teutonic tongues the use of prepositions and of the article has weakened the case endings.' (*Becker, Ausführliche Deutsche Grammatik,* I. 48.)

† 'The relational words have generally originated from notional terms (aus Begriffswörtern), and their derivation from these may still for the most part be shown.' (*Becker,* I. 52.)

of meaning, cannot well be conceived to have taken place at any time. Consequently, if we are now unable to trace any of these so-called particles back to their primitive force, we can only conclude that we are not acquainted with a sufficiently ancient state of the mother-tongue to do so. This view is strengthened by the fact that a large number of them having been already clearly accounted for, argues a like conclusion for the rest, just as a few stones falling to the ground satisfy us that all will if tested. *Through** appears to have been the same originally as the *noun door* in the sense of a *passage* or *medium*. Chaucer writes: 'Idlenesse the *yate* of all harmes, the *thorukke* of all wycked thoughtes,' *i.e.*, as we should say, *through* which they enter. But it cannot be denied that this is very slippery ground, on which more learning and research than sound reasoning have been often expended. The most firmly-established conclusions, such as *if*=*giv*=imperative of *give*=*grant*, have been subsequently shaken, and all that is yet really certain is the general principle here laid down.

THE VOCABULARY—SAXON AND ROMANCE ELEMENTS.

93. The statement that the language has remained unchanged since the middle of the fifteenth century, is true only of its internal structure or grammar. In fixing the date of the modern period no account was or could be taken of the vocabulary, which never is at rest in any living tongue, least of all in English. No people ever absorbed words to anything like the same extent as the English. Insular and ex-

---

* Through is now generally identified with the Aryan root *tar*, entering into the Sanskrit, Greek, and Latin comparatives, and clearly connected with the Latin *trans*. As this *trans* has in its turn become *très* in French, it follows that the expressions *très bon* and *thoroughly good* are originally identical, though we must dig very deeply at the roots of the Aryan stem to recognise their affinity.

clusive in other respects, they are certainly the most cosmopolite of nations in this. All the known languages of the world, living or dead, that they have at any time come in contact with, have contributed to increase their stock of words to such an extent as to render any attempt at complete classification all but impossible. Yet in an historical survey of the one hundred and odd thousand terms contained in the latest dictionaries, a very broad distinction at once presents itself, it being evident that after all the great bulk is made up of *Saxon* and *Romance*. Accessions from all other quarters are too insignificant to be compared with these, and may be safely grouped for the moment under the one head of *miscellaneous*.

Here the Saxon portion claims our attention first, for it is not, indeed, ' so much one element of the English language as the foundation of it, the basis. All its joints, its whole *articulation*, its sinews, and its ligaments, the great body of articles, pronouns, conjunctions, prepositions, numerals, auxiliary verbs, all smaller words which serve to knit together and bind the larger into sentences, these, not to speak of the grammatical structure of the language, are exclusively Saxon '—*English Past and Present*. From which it appears, that in contrasting the two elements, the question of number is of secondary importance, compared with that of the *nature* of the words. Of the 28,000 words in Bosworth's A.S. Dictionary, about 6,000 are supposed to be now obsolete, leaving not more than 22,000—Bosworth says 23,000 —out of 100,000 of Saxon origin—a large balance in favour of the foreign element. Such is, perhaps, the proportion that obtains in dictionaries, where the language is *at rest*, and where a prodigious number of words are enrolled which never existed outside the pages of those works, and of the writers whence they were extracted.

But the comparison should be made by the analysis of sentences, or of the language *in motion*, in order to form a correct notion of the proportion that obtains practically.

Here it is that, on account of the character of the words that are Saxon, the calculation of Trench is really verified. 'Let us suppose the English language to be divided into a hundred parts: of these, to make a rough distribution, *sixty* would be Saxon; *thirty* would be Latin (including of course the Latin which has come to us through the French); *five* would be Greek. We should thus have assigned ninety-five parts, leaving the other five, perhaps too large a residue, to be divided among all the other languages from which we have adopted isolated words.' And in another part of the same admirable lecture upon 'English a Composite Language,' he suggests a good practical test of the great predominance of the Saxon element in composition. We shall find, by experience, that it is all but impossible to put together a single sentence of ordinary length, employing exclusively Latin terms, whereas we may without much strain write whole pages of pure Saxon, without the aid of any foreign words. In fact a logical preposition cannot be uttered in Latin, because the copula is always Saxon. We thus obtain a twofold proportion of

(*a*) Saxon : foreign :: 23 : 77 in dictionaries.
(*b*) Saxon : foreign :: 4 : 1 in the ordinary run of sentences.

PREPONDERANCE OF THE SAXON ELEMENT.

94. And even the preponderance of the foreign over the native element in (*a*) will be considerably modified, when we reflect that it includes not only roots, but a large number of derivatives formed on them by means of Saxon aff- and suffixes: *mis, un, ly, ness, less, ful, ship,* etc. Thus from the Latin *use,* we get *useful, usefully, useless, uselessness;* so *unfortunate, duti-ful, brief-less, falsehood,* words which might, with equal propriety, be classed with the native element. The converse of this, *i.e.* the formation of derivatives on Saxon roots by means of Latin adjuncts, a, ab, pro, ex, al, tion, etc., does not hold as a rule. *Starv-ation* is a curious instance, coined in 1775 by Mr. Dundas, the first Viscount Melville, thence nick-named 'Starvation Dundas.' We say law-*ful*, but leg-*al*, *un*-law-*ful* and *il*-leg-*al*, law-fulness and leg-al-ity. An exception should, however, be made in favour of the ending -*able*, used in such a variety of ways and with such an utter disregard of its original active force: *eatables*, *drinkables*, for things that may be eaten or drunk; *movable*, *allowable*, *sensible*, for senseful, sensitive, and sensible in the expression, 'a *sensible* man; very *sensible* of the cold, and of any *sensible* change in the weather'—*Diversions of Purley*.* The ratio of 23 : 77 is further diminished by the fact, that many of the Saxon words are susceptible of so many different meanings, and of such a variety of applications, that they are often equivalent to four or five distinct terms; so that the whole number, 23, will be employed, on a rough calculation, at least three times oftener than the 77 representing the foreign element. Dr. Withers has illustrated the capabilities of the word *get* by a short specimen, in which it occurs 29 times, nearly always in a different sense, without exhausting its almost endless significations: 'I *got* on horseback after I *got* your letter. When I *got* to Canterbury, I *got* a chaise for town; but I *got* wet through . . *got* such a cold . . to *get* rid of . . *got* shaved . . . *got* into the secret . . . *got* back . . . *got* to bed . . . *got* up . . . *got* down . . . *got* out . . . . *got* home, etc.'

* But such formations date properly from the time of Robert Mannyng (about 1300), who was such a daring innovator in this as in many other respects, and whose writings perhaps mainly on this account assume at times such a surprisingly modern air. Thus he substitutes *crystyanyte* for *cristen-dom*, and writes *bond-age*, which Oliphant instances as 'the first of many words in which a French ending is tacked on to an English root,' p. 246. Later on the practice becomes very frequent, forming a marked feature of the language of Bishop Pecock, who wrote about the middle of the fifteenth century. He is very partial to the ending *able*, forming compounds with it, such as *do-able*, *se-able*, *here-able*, *knowe-able*, &c., that have since been rejected.

THE FOUR PERIODS OF THE ROMANCE ELEMENT.

95. Thus, then, the Latin element, though actually outnumbering the native, is, in reality, of far less importance. The accessions from this source have been divided into the four following periods, which are so far convenient that they point out at once both the time and the nature of the words introduced at different epochs:—

                      A.D.

(*a*) Roman Latin   (1-400) ⎫ explained in Sec. II. § 26.
(*b*) Church Latin (400-1066) ⎭
(*c*) Norman Latin (1066-1450)   ,,   in Sec. IV. § 54 and 55.
(*d*) Book Latin   (1450-1875)

The amount contributed at each of these stages may be represented by the proportions:—

$$a+b : c :: 1 : 100$$
$$a+b+c : d :: 1 : 20$$

That is to say, 100 words were appropriated during the Norman Latin Period, for every one during the two previous taken together; and 20 during the last, or Book Latin Period, for every one during the three previous taken together. In fact, the actual number borrowed directly and indirectly from the Latin throughout the whole of (*d*) is altogether incalculable, if we take into account as well those that have been rejected as those that have been retained. A steady stream of Latinisms was poured into the language with little interruption from the age of Chaucer to that of Gibbon, at some times more copiously than at others, according to the greater or less prevalence of pedantry and learning. It is remarkable that the Scotch carried the practice to the greatest extent, introducing indiscriminately Latin and French words wholesale into their compositions, especially in the fifteenth century, by which they disfigured their own writings without enriching the language. 'The prevailing fault of

English diction in the fifteenth century, is redundant ornament and an affectation of Anglicising Latin words. In this pedantry and use of *aureate terms*, the Scottish versifiers went even beyond their brethren of the South .... When they meant to be eloquent, they tore up words from the Latin, which never took root in the language, like children making a mock garden with flowers and branches stuck in the ground, which speedily wither'—*Campbell in Trench.* Some idea of the length to which the Scotch poets went in this respect may be formed by a passage from the Æneid of Douglas, in the opening of the twelfth book :—

> ' The *auriate* vanes of his throne-soverane
> With glittering glance o'erspread the oceane ;
> The largé fludis leaming all of licht,
> With but ane blink of his *supernal* sicht.
> For to behold it was ane *glore* to see
> The stabled windis and the coloured sea,
> The soft season, the *firmament serene,*
> The lowne *illuminate* air, and firth *amene.*'

Here there are thirteen Latin words, of which the seven in *Italics* were probably coined for the occasion by the poet. The Scottish dialect thus came to be distinguished by two seemingly opposite tendencies, towards the classic tongues in its vocabulary, the Saxon in its grammar (see in this sec., § 86 and 87).

The rage for appropriation prevailed in England principally in the fifteenth century, throughout the Elizabethan age in its greatest extent, and from the Restoration to the death of Gibbon (1794). The wars of Marlborough caused a second accession of French words, chiefly military, of which Addison says in the 'Spectator' (No. 165) :—'The present war has so adulterated our tongue with strange words, that it would be impossible for one of our great-grandfathers to know what his posterity have been doing, were he to read their exploits in a modern newspaper. Our warriors are very industrious in propagating the French language at the same time that they are so gloriously successful in beating down their power.' He instances *reconnoitre, marauder, corps, commandant, pontoon, fascine*, etc., as recent innovations.

CAUSES OF THE COMPOSITE CHARACTER OF MODERN ENGLISH.

96. A variety of causes worked together in rendering the English the most absorbing of all languages. There was first of all the facility and habit acquired by the practice of the Anglo-Norman writers, explained in the last section, § 74 and 75, of which scribblers availed themselves without restraint, introducing an incredible number of foreign words into their writings, through their eagerness to exhibit to the world their ignorance of their own, and their superficial acquaintance with strange tongues. The sort of medley that resulted, and which in times of pedantry passed for fine writing, may be judged of by the style of the following passage in the preface of 'a prose narrative of the adventures of this same Knight of the Swan (*Chevelere de Cigne*), newly translated (1512) out of Frenshe into Englishe at thinstigacion of the puyssaunt and illustryous prynce, lorde Edward, duke of Buckyngham [beheaded 1521]. . . . This highe dygne and illustryous prynce . . . desyrynge cotydially to encrease and augment the name and fame of such as were relucent in virtuous feates and triumphant acts of chyvalry, and to encourage and styre every lusty and genteel herte by the exemplyficacyon of the same, havyng a goodly booke of the highe and miraculous histori of a famous and puyssant kynge named Oryant.' Further on occur the words *ententifly, moiening, cohorted, entendement*, and many hundreds more not now used, but generally current at the time in the works of a class of writers, who ' do greatly seek to stain the language by fond affectation of foreign and strange words, presuming that to be the best English which is most corrupted with external terms of eloquence and sound of many syllables'—*Harrison's Chronicle, Sixteenth Century*. Over 3000 such short-lived terms are to be found in the works of Sir H. Browne and Jeremy Taylor.

Another inducement to borrow largely was the necessity scientific writers and translators were under of finding equivalents for such compound and abstract terms as either never existed in the language, or had disappeared during a long period of neglect. In all cases it was much more expeditious to take the word supplied by the text, drop its inflexions, and give it an English air, by slightly modifying the termination. In this way the early translators of Scripture Anglicised words like *perdition, consolation, reconciliation, sanctification, immortality, transfigure*. A numerous class of theological, philosophical, abstract, and general terms was thus introduced, first into learned works, and then, as these were perused with the spread of general reading, into the current literature, and so familiarised. The number was increased by a natural desire, felt especially by translators, of enriching the language with synonyms and forcible terms, even when corresponding words already existed. In the treatment of elevated subjects, many Normanized Latin words had become too common-place to be any longer available, necessitating a second importation, in a different form, of the same word, or of derivatives direct from the Latin, of previously embodied Norman roots. A curious instance is the Norman *almosine*, filed down through *almosie, almose, almes*, to the monosyllable *alms*, with its seven-syllabled adjective of later date, *eleemosynary*, from the original. The following table will show how abstract derivatives were taken from the Latin, rather than formed on existing Norman and Saxon roots. Some of these thus came to lose the power of further development, as *church, side, hinge*, whilst the adjectives formed on others seemed to lack dignity, though useful in their proper place, *child-like, boyish*, etc. :—

VI.—*Modern English Period.*

church,	ecclesia,	ecclesiastical.	money,	pecunia,	pecuniary.
child,	infans,	infantine.	sun,	sol,	solar.
boy,	puer,	puerile.	parish,	parochia,	parochial.
people,	populus,	populous.	enemy,	inimicus,	inimical.
hinge,	cardo,	cardinal.	chapter,	capitulum,	capitular.
side,	latus,	lateral.	root,	radix,	radical.
kind,	genus,	general-ic.	number,	numerus,	numerous.
isle,	insula,	insular.	mind,	mens,	mental.
dog,	canis,	canine.	knowledge,	scientia,	scientific.
reason,	ratio,	rational.	language,	lingua,	linguistics.

But, perhaps, the greatest cause of all, as that on which those just mentioned were based, was the extremely simple state the language had been reduced to in its structure at the time when the want of a large supply of new words first began to be felt. It is evident that a synthetic language never could become a borrower to any great extent, its numerous inflexions warding off all intruders at whatever point they may wish to force an entrance. Hence the homogeneous character of the classic tongues, and the failure of a large number of Greek terms in attempting to insinuate themselves into Latin, even when taken up by Plautus, Cicero, and others of the greatest weight in literature. *Harpagare* (ἁρπάζω) might read very well, just in one or two tenses or persons, but in others it would appear ridiculous : *harpagabamur, harpagarentur,* etc. ; so *apolactizare, morologus, techna, mastigias,* and others, in Plautus and Terence, refusing to conform themselves to Latin grammar, occasionally also because not required, were ultimately discarded. The Romans were thus compelled to fall back on native sources, just as English writers would have been driven to cultivate the Saxon, had the language preserved any considerable portion of its inflexions when its sphere of action began to be enlarged in the fourteenth century. Then, the Saxon element failing, they would have had recourse to idioms and phrases, such as those employed by the early translators of Scripture, to explain newly-adopted words, or to supply the place of others that could not be embodied : ' I do thankingis to God up on the *unenarrabic,* or, *that may not be told,* gifte of him' (II. *Cor.*, ix.) ; so 'whatever thingis *amyable,* or *able to be lovid*' ; '*swadible, i.e., esi for to trete and to be tretid'* ; 'thou that art *to comynge'* = qui venturus es ; 'that is *to demynge* the quyke and deed' = judicaturus vivos et mortuos, etc., occurring in a version of the N. T. made about 1350. The oneness, or homogeneous character, of the language would have been thus preserved at the expense of the more valuable qualities of boundless wealth and expressiveness. We may conclude that the English never could have become the most composite of all European tongues in its vocabulary, unless it had first become the most analytic in its grammar.

ANALYSIS OF THE ROMANCE ELEMENT IN MODERN ENGLISH.

97. Considered with regard as well to the *manner* as to the *time* of their adoption, the whole body of Latin words may be divided into four classes. Some, principally relating to church matters, were introduced in Saxon times. These were, therefore, first *Saxonized*: episcopus=bisceop=bishop (*a*). Some in Norman times, and therefore *Normanized*: amabilis=aimable=amiable (*b*). Some during the modern period direct, and simply *Anglicized*: homicida=homicide (*c*). Some recently, chiefly technical, without any change: postulata (*d*). A few have actually undergone all these processes, as:—

(*a*)			(*d*)
predicare	précneur	prædicare,	prædicata.
predician	preacher	predicate,	prædicata.
sanctus,	sanctifier	sanctitas,	S. sanctorum.
sanct,	sanctify,	sanctity,	S. sanctorum.
candela,	chandlier,	candelabrum,	candelabra.
candel,	chandler,	candelabrums,	candelabra.

It should, however, be observed, with regard to most of these Saxonized words, that the orthography of their present equivalents proves them to be a later importation through the Norman, not a modification of the older forms. *Munk* may be from *munuc*, *priest* from *preost*, but *porch* is evidently the Norman *porche*, not the Saxon *portic* ; *parsley* from *persil* rather than from *peterselige*; so *saint, preach*, perhaps *chalice* (see § 26).

Several have gone through the first three changes, as :—

(a)	(b)	(c)
{ clauster, cluster,	cloitre, cloister,	claustrum. claustral.
{ pæl, pall,	palliatif, palliative,	pallium. pallium.
{ munuc, munk,	monachisme, monachism,	monachus. monachal.
{ mynster, minster,	monastère, monastery (?)	monasticus. monastic.
{ mæsse, mass,	missive, missive,	missalis. missal.

Some of these are doubtful, nor is it always possible to say whether a word is from the Norman or Latin, *monastery* from *monastère* or *monasterium*, *liberty* from *liberté* or *libertas*, *nation* from *nation* or *natio*. Of course, if current in Norman and Early English times, the presumption will be in favour of a Norman origin, though many such terms were even then introduced direct from the Latin by translators from Latin works, especially Trevisa and Wickliff.

Others have passed through the three last stages, as :—

(b)	(c)	(d)	(b)	(c)	(d)
ray,	radious,	radii.	indicant,	indexes,	indices.
radiant,	radiate,	radiata.	nebule,	nebulous,	nebulæ.
radish,	radical,	radices.	genial,	geniuses,	genii
addition,	add,	addenda.	general,	generate,	genera.
errant,	error,	errata.			

And a vast number through (b) and (c), always with a difference of meaning, thus contributing with their Saxon equivalents to the unequalled resources of the language in expressing the nicer shades of thought. The following list bears out, on the whole, the rule which has been laid down, that ' if a word be directly from the Latin, it will not have undergone any alteration or modification in its form and shape, save only as respects the termination : " innocentia " will have become " innocency," " natio " will have become " nation," " firmamentum," " firmament," but nothing more. On the other hand, if it comes *through* the French, it will generally be considerably altered in its passage. It will have undergone a process of lubrication; its sharply-defined Latin outline will in good part have departed from it; thus "crown" is from "corona," but through "couronne," and itself a dissyllable, "coroune" in our earlier English; "treasure" is from "thesaurus," but through "trésor"; "emperor" is the Latin "imperator," but it was first "empereur"'—*E. Past and Present*, I. It also illustrates what is often found to be the case, that the Saxon element is the more poetic, the Norman the more available for ordinary purposes, and the Latin the more scientific. There is poetry in *beam*: 'Smiling through pleasure's beam,' or, 'As a beam o'er the face of the waters,' where *ray* would be intolerable. But we talk in prose of the *rays* of the sun, and in science of the *radii* of a circle.

Saxon.	Norman.	Latin.	Saxon.	Norman.	Latin.
lawful,	loyal,	legal.	weak,	frail,	fragile.
kingly,	royal,	regal.	try,	prove,	probe.
deadly,	mortal,	mortiferous.	wedlock,	marriage,	matrimony.
trust,	fealty,	fidelity.	ghost,	sprite,	spirit.
tithe,	dime,	decimal.	fearful,	horrible,	horrid.
beam,	ray,	radius.	clever,	adroit,	dexterous.
leader,	chief,	captain.	bold,	valiant,	valorous.
wonder,	marvel,	miracle.	atonement,	ransom,	redemption.
ox,	beef,	bovine.	first,	prime,	primary.
strength,	force,	fortitude.	feeling,	sense,	sensation.
wise,	sage,	sapient.	shorten,	abridge,	abbreviate.
old,	ancient,	antiquated	to lower,	to humble,	to humiliate.

SYNONYMS.

98. Some of the words in this list, which might be extended to any length, approach very nearly to what are called perfect synonyms. The question of the actual existence of such in any language should perhaps be decided, as metaphysicians have decided that of the possible existence of two or more objects perfectly similar without being identical, *i.e.*, solo numero differentia. Intrinsece non repugnant, ergo extrinsece possibilia, sed non dantur. So that, though such terms may be conceived as possible, practically they do not exist. The reason is because ideas being vastly more numerous than words, it would lack common sense to bestow more than one equivalent on any given notion, while so many others are left unprovided for. Hence one term may often stand for a multiplicity of things, but no one thought will ever possess more than one term to express it accurately. In English there are Saxon and Latin words etymologically the same, yet, perhaps, never quite identical in meaning. *Yearlings* are not *annuals*; so may be compared *felicity* and *happiness*, *Godhead* and *divinity*, *earth* and *soil*, *anger* and *indignation*, *rabble* and *mob* (mobile), *huge* and *vast*, *great* and *large*, *stream* and *river*; though it would be difficult to say in what lies the difference between *rivulet* and *brooklet*, or *brook* and *streamlet*. Locke does not point it out when he says: ' *springs* make little *rivulets*, and these united form *brooks*, which coming forward in *streams*, compose great *rivers* that run into the sea.' Perhaps all comprised would flow thus: spring, rillet, rill, rivulet, brooklet, brook, streamlet, stream, river. So great is the demand for words, that a mere difference of spelling or of termination is often sufficient to constitute a wide difference of meaning. *Desk* and *dish* were originally one (*disc*); so were *skirt* and *shirt*, *black* and *bleak*. Compare also *bountiful* and *bounteous*, *joyful* and *joyous*, *changeful* and *changing*, *diamond* and *adamant*, *captive* and *caitiff*, *scandal* and *slander*, *spirit* and *sprite*, *human* and *humane*, *gentle* and *genteel*, and many others cited by Trench, who truly observes that the subject is inexhaustible (*E. Past and Present*, II.)

GREEK ELEMENT.

99. Out of the hundred parts into which the vocabulary has been distributed, ten being reserved for the *miscellaneous* (§ 93), five of these will be absorbed by the Greek. Words from this source are either *indirect* through the Latin and Norman, as *bishop, monk, priest, monastery*, already discussed under those heads, or *direct* in modern times, generally scientific and technical. Of the latter, some have conformed to the rules of English grammar, though not always without a struggle: ἐγκυκλοπαίδεια (*B. Jonson*), later on 'encyclopedia,' and now 'cyclopedia'; others have retained their proper plural endings, either because very recently adopted: apsis, pl. apsides; or through some unaccountable caprice: κριτήριον was new to J. Taylor, for he so writes it, but old enough now to have long ago laid aside its still retained pl. 'criteria.' The retention of these plurals is not always a sure test of the time of adoption, either in Latin or Greek: phenomenon -na, datum -ta, erratum -ta, are very old, and it is a mistake to suppose that all such terms passed through this process of gradual conformation to the genius of the language. 'Lipothymy,' if used only by J. Taylor, was never written λειποθυμία, but Anglicised at once with hundreds of others, some surviving, some long since dead, at a time of indiscriminate appropriation.

MISCELLANEOUS ELEMENT.

100. Words from all other sources, making up the five remaining parts, may be generally described as sporadic, a few scattered terms here and there, in the collection of which writers on the English language have often displayed more research than discernment. Thus *cherub* and *Gehenna* are placed in the same category of words from the Hebrew. Surely some distinction should be drawn between two such terms as these. No word can be said to be properly embodied, unless it has acquired some little power of generalization over and above its individual meaning, otherwise no distinction is observed between *proper* nouns and *common*. *Cherub* is clearly an instance of Hebrew adoption; we call a pretty child a *cherub*; so are *shibboleth, seraph, sabbath,* but *Gehenna* seems to have about as much right to be considered English as any other *proper name, Verona, Timbuctoo*. It answers strictly to the definition given by grammarians of a *proper* noun, and to no other: 'proper nouns express *particular* persons or places' (*Bromby*), and we might add *things*. *Muslin*, no doubt, may be cited, as a word taken from Hindostanee, but not *lac*, until it shall come to mean something more than a particular sum of a particular coin peculiar to India. A word is not naturalized so long as it is employed to denote only special foreign things, without further extension of meaning. Words like *hallelujah, amen, razzia, sahara, chimpanzee*, are therefore excluded from the subjoined list of a few, out of many, cited by Trench and others. They are here arranged according to the proportion each language seems to have contributed. Arabic is placed first, because the words it has supplied are really more important than all the rest put together:—

ARABIC.—Admiral, alchemy, alcohol, alcove, alembic, algebra, alkali, almanac, amber, amulet, arrack, arsenal, artichoke, assassin, atlas, azimuth, azure, bazaar, camphor, carat, chemistry, cipher, coffee, cotton, crimson, dragoman, elixir, gazelle, giraffe, lemon, lime, magazine, nadir, saffron, shrub, syrup, talisman, tariff, zenith, zero.

ITALIAN.—Balcony, balustrade, bandit, bravo, bust, canto, caricature, carnival, charlatan, ditto, folio, gazette, grotto, harlequin, influenza, motto, parapet, pianoforte, portico, regatta, sonnet, stanza, stucco, studio, umbrella, virtuoso, vista, zany.

SPANISH.—Alligator, barricade, bravado, cargo, cigar, don, flotilla, gala, grenade, hooker, jennet, merino, parasol, punctilio, sherry, verandah.

DUTCH.—Boom, boor, cruise, scamper, schooner, skates, skipper, sloop, smuggle, stiver, taffrel, wear (*veer*), yacht.

GERMAN.—Cobalt, felspar, loafer, nickel, quartz, waltz, watershed, zinc.

PERSIAN.—Chess*, indigo, lilac, orange, sash, shawl, sherbet, shrub, sofa, tambour, turban.

* Chaturanga (Sanscrit), chatrang (Pers.), shatranj (Arab), scacchi (Ital.), échecs (French), check, and chess. *Pawn* is the Indian *peon*, a

TURKISH.—Caftan, divan, janissary, odalisk, sash, tulip, perhaps scimitar and civet.

HINDOSTANEE.—Calico, chintz, cowrie, dimity, jungle, loot, muslin, palanquin, pundit, rum, rice, toddy.

CHINESE.—Caddy, mandarin, nankeen, satin, tea.

AMERICAN.—Canoe, chocolate, cocoa, hamoc, maize, potato (batata), tobacco, tomata, wigwam, yam.

STYLE—GENERIC AND SPECIFIC TERMS—PLATITUDES.

101. There are some few words from the Malay, Hebrew, and other tongues; but it is obvious that the whole of this *miscellaneous* department is as nothing compared with the Saxon and Latin elements, and is of no account in any question of style. Latin having furnished many duplicates or synonyms of Saxon words, it will be important to consider the nature of each class, in order to decide on our selection, wherever we have the option of choice. The subjoined scheme will show that the Latin words are abstract and generic, the Saxon concrete and specific; and as it is a law of style that it is the more animated and vigorous, in proportion to the prevalence of the latter, it follows, that, other considerations being equally balanced, the Saxon will be the better word of the two. It is always more accurate, and in nine cases out of ten more desirable, to use specific than generic words, but also more difficult; accordingly, careless and superficial writers are full of platitudes, and platitudes are Latin.

Affections in General.	*Kinds of Feeling.*	*Motion in General.*	*Kinds of Movement.*
impression	warmth	impulse	thrust
sensation	thrill	direction	steer
emotion	flurry	progression	brisk
disposition	mildness	ascension	climb
temper	heat	descent	roll

foot soldier. *Rook* is doubtful, either the Pers. *rohk*, a camel bearing archers, or the Sanscrit *rat'h*, *rot'h*, corrupted to *rohk* by the Persians, an armed chariot (*Sir W. Jones*).

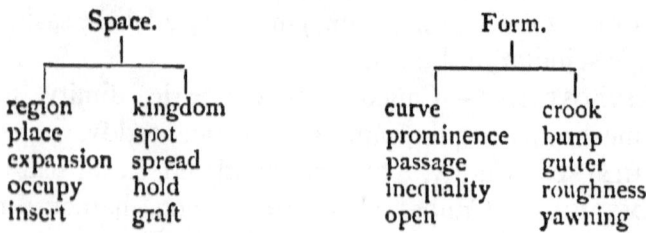

Thus, it will be better to speak of the *warmth* or *glow* of one's feelings, than of his *profound impressions*; to thrust, push, or drag forward, than simply to impel; to climb the tree, rather than ascend it; to graft on it rather than insert. If a thing is curved, it is curved in some way, either crooked, or hooked, or arched; these words are, therefore, more graphic. The use of the others habitually is a mark of a barren mind in the individual, a symptom of decay in general literature.*

Whether modern English writers exhibit any such symptoms by too great fondness for Latin words, may be best judged of in the following comparative table, drawn up by Turner in his 'Hist. of the A.S.,' on an analysis of passages from the different authors included in it. The figures in the

---

* The whole subject is ably handled in Chapter VI. of Oliphant's 'Standard English,' where he proposes the three following sentences in illustration of a plain Saxon, an ordinary Norman, and an inflated Latin style:—

I. Stung by the foe's twitting, our forefathers (bold wights!) drew nigh their trusty friends, and were heartily welcomed; taught by a former mishap, they began the fight on that spot, and showed themselves unaffrighted by threatening forebodings of woe.

II. Provoked by the enemies' abuse, our ancestors (brave creatures!) approached their faithful allies, and were nobly received; instructed by a previous misfortune, they commenced the battle in that place, and proved themselves undismayed by menacing predictions of misery.

III. Exacerbated by the antagonist's vituperations, our progenitors (audacious individuals!) approximated to their reliable auxiliaries, and were ovated with empressement: indoctrinated by a preliminary contretemps, they inaugurated hostilities in that locality, and demonstrated themselves as unintimidated by minatory vaticinations of catastrophe.

left-hand column show the whole number of words in each extract, and those in the right-hand, the number which are foreign or not Saxon :—

Genesis, } Ang. Bible {	128	5
John, xi.	74	2
Spenser	72	14
Shakespeare	83	13
Milton	89	16
Cowley	77	10
Thomson	78	14
Addison	79	15
Locke	94	20
Pope	83	27
Young	96	21
Swift	90	10
Robertson	113	34
Hume	101	37
Gibbon	79	32
Johnson	81	21
	1427	291

The mean proportion not Saxon is about one-fifth, the Anglican Bible and Gibbon occupying the two extremes. The list, of course, includes no names of the present century, during which a reaction has set in that has stopped all further pilferings from the Latin, except for scientific purposes. It being impossible to revive obsolete A.S. words, and difficult to compound English, Carlyle and his school have shown Germanic tendencies, even in their style, just as Milton often wrote Greek and Latin sentences with English words : 'and knew not eating death,' *i.e.*, οὐκ ἔγνω θάνατον φάγουσα (B. IX). Oh, miserable of happy (X.) ; How cam'st thou, speakable of mute? (IX.) All the different styles which have at any time prevailed may be reduced to four :—

SAXON.—Cynewulf, Alfred, Layamon, Orrmin, Tyndale, the English Bible, Swift, De Foe, Bunyan, Burns, Coleridge, Cobbett, Carlyle, Tennyson, Morris (especially in 'The Earthly Paradise').

VI.—*Modern English Period.*

NORMAN.—Robert of Gloucester, Robert Manning, William Langland, Chaucer, Gower, Dryden, Goldsmith.
LATIN.—Taylor, Milton, Sir Thomas Browne, the Douay Bible, Dr. Johnson, Robertson, Gibbon.
MEDIUM.—Mandeville, Spenser, Shakespeare, Addison, Pope, Scott, Byron, Moore, Froude, Longfellow, and moderns generally.

PRESENT POSITION AND FUTURE PROSPECTS OF THE ENGLISH LANGUAGE.

102. Throughout the whole of the last century, French was the general medium of intercourse in Europe, and at one time seemed destined to become the universal language of literature. Germans wrote in French, as the Russians still frequently do; and a hundred years have scarcely elapsed since Gibbon purposed employing it in the composition of his great work, the 'Decline and Fall,' published between the years 1776 and 1788. He was dissuaded from doing so by the advice of David Hume, who foresaw in the countless colonies and dependencies of the crown of England, the future ascendancy of the English language. The rapid growth of these colonies has already verified Hume's prediction, and at the present day English is the most universally diffused language on the globe, being the general speech of the British Isles, Australia, Van Diemen's Land, New Zealand, South Africa, and all North America, except Mexico; or, in other words, the mother tongue of nearly one hundred millions of human beings. In this last respect the subjoined table will show that it falls short of Chinese and perhaps of Hindostanee, which, as the universal medium of communication in India, is generally spoken by all classes, with little dialectic variety. Though Chinese is split up into a great many varieties, yet the literary standard is known everywhere, and probably understood by as many as is here stated. Russian is restricted to the pure Russian population, though generally diffused throughout the empire. In point of extent, it ranks next to English, reaching from St. Petersburg to

Behring's Straits. French includes the French-speaking populations of Belgium and North America. Arabic is the most widely spread, next to the Russian, stretching without interruption from the shores of the Atlantic, through Barbary and Egypt, to the Persian frontier, and including Syria and Mesopotamia, besides Arabia Proper. In this rough estimate no account could be taken of the extent to which any of these languages may be known outside the country, French in Russia, English in India. The really educated in any country are comparatively few; and experience tells us that the French current outside France has not greatly improved since the days of Chaucer (see § 71):—

Chinese . . 300,000,000	Russian . . 45,000,000
Hindostanee . . 100,000,000	French . . 40,000,000
English . . 90,000,000	Arabic . . 35,000,000
German . . 50,000,000	Japanese . . 30,000,000

It has been calculated that before the close of the century English will be spoken by about 200,000,000 of people, but whether in its integrity, or with differences of dialect by the populations of the future empires of America and Australia, is a question it would be idle here to discuss. It may be observed, however, that, notwithstanding the powerful action of climate, society, and other external causes, it is hard to believe that distinctly new forms of speech will arise for many ages, directly opposed as they would be to the interests of commerce, education, literature, the free intercourse of man with man,—in a word, of civilization. A common speech has ever been felt to be an advantage. When, therefore, a large portion of the human family find themselves blessed with such a boon, they will instinctively endeavour to retain possession of it. That any change in the present state of the English tongue would be a falling off, rather than an improvement, may be argued from the remarkable words of a foreigner, Jacob Grimm, with which this work may be fittingly concluded. He observes that it possesses

VI.—*Modern English Period.*

'A veritable power of expression, such as perhaps never stood at the command of any other language of men. . . . Its highly spiritual genius, and wonderfully happy development and condition, have been the result of a surprisingly intimate union of the two noblest languages in modern Europe, the Teutonic and the Romance. It is well known in what relation these two stand to one another in the English tongue, the former supplying in far larger proportion the material groundwork, the latter the spiritual conceptions. In truth, the English language, which by no mere accident has produced and upborne the greatest and most predominant poet of modern times, as distinguished from the ancient classical poetry (I can, of course, only mean Shakespeare), may, with all right, be called a world-language, and, like the English people, appears destined hereafter to prevail with a sway more extensive even than its present, over all the portions of the globe. For in wealth, good sense, and closeness of structure, no other of the languages at this day spoken deserves to be compared with it, not even our German, which is torn, even as we are torn, and must first rid itself of many defects, before it can enter boldly into the lists, as a competitor with the English.'—Quoted in 'E. Past and Present,' I.

QUESTIONS.

79. Who is the first Modern English writer? Show that the Old E. forms occurring in him, and others of the time, are no argument that the structure of the language was not completely formed about 1450.

80. What is the state of the language of the poets connecting Chaucer with Surrey, 1400—1516? of the Scottish ballad poetry? of the Northumbrian?

81. Caxton's orthography proves that the chief difference between Middle and Modern E. had disappeared when he wrote? Who is the first *idiomatic* E. writer?

82. Explain the *conservative* effects of the introduction of printing.

83. What was its action on the orthography? The irregular spelling of *stewardship*, *rich*, *it*, . . . in the sixteenth century proves that the pronunciation was uniform and much the same as now?

84. Explain the three great sources of the present inconsistent state of the orthography. What was Euphuism? In what did it effect a permanent change? How far is the present alphabet inadequate to express the actual sounds of the spoken language?

85. How many A.S. grammatical forms survive? Have these been

increased by accessions from the French or Latin? Contrast English as an analytic language with the other European tongues.

86. In the comparative table, the forms *boces* and *bokis* imply a change of alphabet: *cildra* and *childer*, a change of pronunciation: béc and boces, cycenu and cicenes, a general substitution of *es* for all the A.S. plurals?

[An indefinite number of questions of this sort will be suggested by a careful study of this table.]

87-88. Is *chicken* the pl. of *chick*? Does the A.S. pl. in *an* account for the *n* in *children*, *kine*, &c.? Are there any surviving representatives of that pl.? Several Old E. plurals in *en*, not found in the A.S., seem to confirm Higden's statement of the existence in his time of three great English dialects, and that the present standard has resulted from the blending of two of these, rather than been derived direct from the A.S. literary standard?

89-90. Account for the form *its* for *his*. When did the change occur? Account for *th* in they, them; for hí, heom. Though only appearing in Modern E. these forms are probably older than the A.S.?

91. Explain the *s*, third pers. sing., pres. *loves* for *loveth*. Show that *-ing* and *-ed* are improperly called participles *present* and *past*. What are they?

92. How far do the relational words or particles answer to the logical definition of a *term* as distinguished from a mere *vox*?

93-94. In estimating the proportion of Saxon and Latin in the vocabulary, what consideration is the most important? Of the whole number of words how many are A.S.? Latin? Miscellaneous?

95. Classify the Latin element. State the ratios, showing the relative amount introduced at different times. The Scotch dialect exhibits two opposite tendencies? In modern times, at what several epochs was Latin appropriated most extensively?

96. Explain the first reason why English is the most absorbing of all languages. Are all the words borrowed from the Latin now retained? The second reason? Account for a second importation of the same word, and for Latin adjectives of Saxon nouns, *hinge*, *cardinal*. The third reason? Show that the present composite state of the vocabulary is preferable to one less mixed.

97-98. What four processes have Latin words gone through? Are all the modern representatives of the Saxonized words derived from them? The same word may have gone through all, or some of these processes? How are the Normanized distinguishable from the Anglicized? Are perfect synonyms impossible? Why do they not exist?

VI.—Modern English Period.

99-100. The Greek element is two-fold? Some Greek words retain their proper pl. endings. Is this a test of the *time* of their adoption? With regard to words from other sources, what distinction is to be observed? What languages have contributed most?

101. Saxon words are *specific*, Latin *generic*. Which should be preferred where we have the option of choice? Why? Classify writers according to the prevalence of one or other element in their works.

102. What is the present position of the English language, as to general diffusion? Numbers that speak it? Its future destiny?

APPENDIX I.

CONTAINING TWELVE VERSIONS OF THE LORD'S PRAYER FROM THE EIGHTH TO THE SIXTEENTH CENTURY.

I.

About 750.

From a MS. printed in Whelock's 'Bede,' p. 495, and preceded by this curious little rubrick: 'Her is geleafa, and gebed, and bletsung, læwedum mannum ðe þæt Leden ne cunnon,' *i.e.* Here is the Belief, and Prayer, and Blessing, for lay men, they that can not Latin.

II.

About 880.

From Mareschall and Junius' 'Saxon Gospels.'

III.

About 975.

In the Northumbrian dialect, from the 'Rushworth Gloss.'

IV.

About 1130.

From the celebrated 'Psalter' in Trinity College, Cambridge, referred by Wanley to the reign of Stephen. Note here the disappearance of many strong endings, a more modern arrangement of the words, and the substitution of *give* for *syllan*, which originally meant not *to sell*, but *to give*. But Normanisms are still absent.

V.

About 1175.

A poetic version, from a MS. sc.t by Adrian IV. to England during the reign of Henry II.

VI.

About 1200.

From a MS. in Trinity College, Cambridge, 'Wanley,' p. 169.

VII.

About 1250.

Also in rhyme. Here for the first time we find traces of Normanisms in the words *dettes* and *detturs*. The grammar and order of words are modern.

VIII.

About 1280.

From a MS. of the thirteenth century, printed in the 'Reliquiæ Antiquæ,' i. 22—apparently in the East Midland, or perhaps Northumbrian dialect.

IX.

About 1380.

This is from Wycutt's version, completed in the reign of Richard II. It contains five Romance terms: substaunce, dettis, dettouris, temptacioun, and *delyvere*.

X.

About 1430.

From a Bodleian MS. said to have been given by Henry VI. to the Carthusians in London. It seems, like all subsequent versions, to be based on that of Wycliff.

XI.

About 1500.

From the 'Liber Festialis.'

XII.

1526.

From Tyndale's Version.

Twelve Versions of the Lord's Prayer

1. Du ure Fæder, ðe eart on heofenum.
2. Fæder ure þu, þe eart on heofenum.
3. Fæder ure þu, þe in heofonum earð.
4. Fader ure, þe art on heofone.
5. Ure fadyr in heaven rich ;
6. Fader ure, thu ert in hevene.
7. Fadir ur, that es in hevene,
8. Ure fadir, þat hart in hevene,
9. Our Fadir, that art in hevenys ;
10. Oure fadir, that art in hevenes ;
11. Fader eure, that arte in hevynes ;
12. Our Father, which art in heaven ;

1. Sy ðin nama gehalgod.
2. Si þin nama gehalgod.
3. Beo gehalgud þin noma.
4. Sy gebletsod name þin,
5. ðy name be hallyed everlich ;
6. Bledsed be thi name.
7. Halud thi nam to nevene ;
8. Halged be þi name with giftis sevene :
9. Halewid be thi name ;
10. Halewid be thi name ;
11. Halowed be thy name ;
12. Halowed be thy name ;

1. Gecume þin rice.
2. To becume þin rice.
3. Cume to þine rice.
4. Cume þin rike.
5. ðou bring us thy micheli blisse ;
6. Cume thi rixlenge.
7. Thou do as thi rich rike ;
8. Samin (also) cume þi Kingdom,
9. Thi kingdom come to ;
10. Thi kingdom come to thee ;
11. Thy kingdom come ;
12. Let Thy kingdom come ;

1. Sy ðin willa swa swa on heofenum swa eac on eorþan.
2. Gewurðe þin willa on eorþan swa swa on heofenum.

3. Weorðe þin willa swa swa on heofune swilc on eorðe.
4. Si þiu wil swa swa on heofone and on eorþan.
5. Als hit in heaven y-doe,
    Evar in yearth beene it also.
6. Wurthe thi wil on eorthe swo it is on hevene.
7. Thi will on erd be wrought eek, as it is wrought in heven ay.
8. Þi wille in herþe als in hevene be don,
9. Be thi wil done in erthe, as in hevene.
10. Be thi wil don in eerthe, as in hevene.
11. Thy wyl be doon in erth, as it is in hevyn.
12. Thy will be fulfilled as well in earth as it is in heven.

1. Syle us to dæg urne dæghwomlican hlaf.
2. Urne dæghwamlicam hlaf syle us to dæg.
3. Hlaf userne dæghwamlicu sel us to dæg.
4. Breod ure degwamlich *geof* us to dæg.
5. Ðat holy bread that lasteth aye,
    Ðou send it ous this ilke day.
6. Gif us todai ure daigwamliche bread.
7. Ur ilk day brede give us to day.
8. Ure bred þat lastes ai, give it hus this hilke dai;
9. Give to us this day oure breed ovir othir *substaunce*,
10. Give to us this day oure breed over othre substance;
11. Our every daies brede gyve us to daye;
12. Geve us this day ur dayly bred,

1. And forgif us ure gyltas swa swa we forgyfaþ ðam ðe wiþ us agyltaþ.
2. And forgyf us ure gyltas swa swa we forgifað urum gyltendum.
3. And forlete us ure scylde swa swa we ec forleten þæm þe scyldigat wiþ us.
4. And forgeof us ageltes ura swa swa we forgeofen agiltendum urum.
5. Forgiue ous all that we have done
    As we forgiuet uch other mon.
6. And forgiue us ure gultes swo we don hem here the us agult.
7. Forgive thou all us *dettes* urs, als we forgive till ur *detturs*.
8. And ure misdedis þu forgyve hus, als we forgyve þam þat misdon hus;
9. And forgive to us our *dettis*, as we forgiven to oure *dettouris*.
10. And forgive us our dettis, as we forgiven oure dettouris;
11. And forgive us our trespasses as we forgyve theym that trespasse agaynste us:
12. And forgeve us oure dettes as we forgeve ur detters.

1. And ne læd ðu na us on costnunge.
2. And ne gelædde þu us on costnunge.
3. And ne gelæt us geleade in costnungæ.
4. And ne led us on costunge.
5. Ne let ous fall into no foundung.
6. Habbeth shild us fram elche pine of helle.
7. And ledde us in na fandung.
8. And leod us intol na fandinge ;
9. And lede us not into *temptacioun* ;
10. And lede us not into temptation,
11. And lede us not in temptacion,
12. And leade us not into temptation,

1. Ac alys us fram yfele.   Sy hit swa.
2. Ac alys us of yfele.   Soþlice.
3. Ah gelese us of yfle.   Amen.
4. Ac alys us fram yfele.   Swa beo hit.
5. Ac shield ous fro the fowle þing.   Amen.
6. Ac les us of alle iuele.   Amen.   Swo it wurthe.
7. But sculd us fra ivel thing.   Amen.
8. Bot frels us fra alle ivele þinge.   Amen.
9. But *delyvere* us from yvel.   Amen.
10. But delivere us from ivel.   Amen.
11. But delyver us from all evyll.   Amen.
12. But delyver us from evyll.   For thyne is the kyngdom, and the power, and the glorye, for ever.   Amen.

APPENDIX II.

A DIGEST OF EARLY ENGLISH REMAINS FROM BEOWULF TO MANNING.

ANGLO-SAXON PERIOD : 450-1066.

(Pagan and Continental.)

BEOWULF : an alliterative epic, 6,350 short lines—prehistoric, but committed to writing in Christian times—one MS. Cott. Vitellius A. 15, fol. 130-198—referred to tenth century, injured by the fire in Brit. Mus. 1731, probably represents the West Saxon speech of seventh century, first published by G. J. Thorkelin, Copenhagen, 1815. In present form say . 650

(Best ed. Grein's, in his *Bibliothek der A.S. Poesie*, i. 1857.)

FINNESBURG : a war-song, pre-historic, fragmentary, 48 lines, discovered by Hickes on the cover of a MS. of Homilies in Lambeth Lib. and published in his Thesaurus Ling. Vet. Sept. 1703-5 650

DEOR'S COMPLAINT : partly epic and partly lyrical, in strophes, probably composed on the Mainland—in the Exeter MS., 42 lines, Grein ed. vol. I. 650

WIDSIÐ = *The Wide Wanderer* : a descriptive poem. If the 'Wanderer' be a real character, may be referred to A. 375, d. of Eormenric, King of the Goths, visited by him. Otherwise pre-historic and legendary. In the Exeter MS., ed. Grein, I. 143 lines 650

(Christian.)

CADMON : of him genuine : 'Hymn on the Creation,' a scrap, referred to by Beda, 'Eccl. Hist.' IV. 24, and embodied in a West-Saxon form in Alfred's version of that work ; but a Northumbrian MS., Bodl. C. C. C. ? referred to tenth century, possibly preserves the original text, died . . . 680

To him also referred : POETICAL PARAPHRASE OF GENESIS, 2,935 lines ; of *Exodus*, 589 lines ; of Daniel, 765 lines ; and portions of N. T.—all extant in a Southern form, in one MS., Bodl. Jun. XI., referred to tenth century, first published by Junius, Amsterdam, 1655, again by Thorpe, 1832, and Grein, I. 1857. If at all composed by the Northumbrian Cadmon, has been materially altered by Southern transcribers—present text seems to represent the West Saxon speech of eighth century, say 750

To him the poem of 'THE HOLY ROOD, A DREAM,' 87 lines, in the Vercelli MS. (21 lines of which also in Runes on the Ruthwell Cross, first deciphered by Kemble), is wrongly attributed by George Stephens, who reads the head Rune :

ᚳᚪᛞᛗᚩᚾ ᛗᚫ ᚠᚪᚢᛖᚦᚩ

Cadmon mæ fauepo = Cadmon me fawed (made). But this may refer perhaps to the engraver, or designer of the Cross, certainly not to the author of the poem, who seems to have been CYNEWULF, here-under mentioned, and who composed it as an introduction to the longer poem of the ELENE (undoubtedly by him) which follows it in the Vercelli MS., and in the epilogue expressly alludes to it . . . . 800?

THE JUDITH : a religious epic, in 12 cantos, of which last three only extant, in same MS. as the *Beowulf*, fol. 199—350 lines, probably the very finest piece of A.S. poetry extant— author unknown—almost certainly not Cadmon, although attributed to him by Stephens on what he calls internal evidence, a phrase often meaning nothing more reliable than the critic's inner consciousness. Grein ed., vol. I. Language West Saxon, somewhat more recent than the paraphrases, say . 800

CYNEWULF : name certain, being worked in acrostic fashion into some of his longer pieces—identity not settled ; neither a bishop of Lindisfarne (d. 780), nor an abbot of Peterborough (d. 1014), as has been supposed, but probably a Northumbrian minstrel (and consequently a layman) of eighth or ninth century, though all his works are extant in a Southern form. They are contained partly in the Vercelli, and partly in the Exeter Codex.

Thus in the Vercelli : His *Elene*, or Finding of the True Cross, 1,321 lines in Grein's ed., Vol. II. ; THE ADVENTURES OF ST. ANDREW amongst the cannibal Marmedonians, 1,724 lines (of which conclusion defective, but probably contained his name in Acrostics); and THE HOLY ROOD above mentioned under Cadmon. As the short extract from this in Runes on the Ruthwell Cross is in the Northumbrian speech, we may conclude that all his writings were originally composed in this dialect, and that, as stated, Cynewulf was a North countryman, the forerunner of the long race of Northern minstrels that have not yet ceased to sing.

In the Exeter MS. his Legend of ST. JULIANA, who suffered under Maximinian, 731 lines; his CHRIST, a series of hymns on the threefold coming of Christ, 1,694 lines; and a collection of riddles or charades elegantly turned.

There are several other lyrical pieces in the Exeter MS. which from their style seem also to be the work of Cynewulf. Such are: THE LIFE OF ST. GUÐLAC, 1,353 lines; THE PHŒNIX, 677 lines; THE WANDERER, 115 lines; THE SEAFARER, 124 lines; THE WIFE'S COMPLAINT, 53 lines; and the striking fragment of THE RUIN, 47 lines. These shorter lyrical pieces, if by him, are much superior to his longer works, and entitle him to the highest rank among Anglo-Saxon poets. All are published by Grein, Vols. I. and II., and may be referred to . . 800–850

THE NORTHUMBRIAN PSALTER, in the Rushworth Gospels, IV. Prolegomena, CIX. (Surtees Society), referred by Garnett to 800

PSALMS 51 to 150, metrical, MS. Bibl. Paris, of eleventh century, but Dietrich (apud Grein) says that this version 'Vielleicht dem Aldhelm zuzuschreiben sei' (II. 412) . . . 800?

PSALMS 1 to 50, in prose, same MS. as foregoing, probably composed in eleventh century to complete the Psalter, or to replace lost metrical originals. All edited by Thorpe, Oxford, 1835, and Grein, Vol. II.

PSALM L. Cott. Vesp. D. VI. ed. Grein, Vol. II.

ALFRED'S writings: a free version of OROSIUS, with important additions. A close translation of BEDA'S ECCL. HIST.; an enlarged version of BOETHIUS, '*de Consolatione Philosophiæ*,' the poetical portions of which are published separately by Grein, Vol. II., and his translation of Pope Gregory's REGULA PASTORALIS, extant in three contemporary MSS. : Bodl. Hatt. 20; Cott. Tib. B. XI. (best text); and Cott. Otho B. II. The first two (collated with the third) printed by

Henry Sweet, Oxford, 1871, for the Early English Text   870
Society 900

THE SAXON CHRONICLE: a national record, retrospective from J. Cæsar till the reign of Alfred (by whom probably originated), thenceforth till death of Stephen (1154), contemporary, or nearly so, with some forgeries, for which see below, ad A. 1120. Extant mainly in six MSS. more or less perfect, and breaking off at various dates:—

I. The Plegemund, Corp. Cam. LXXIII. The Saxon portion ending in 1070.
II. Cotton Tib. A. VI., ending 977.
III. Cott. Tib. B. I., ending 1066.
IV. Cott. Tib. B. IV., ending 1079.
V. Cott. Dom. A. VIII., ending 1058, in Saxon and Latin.
VI. Bodl. Laud E. 80, ending 1154.

Inserted at various dates are sundry short poems, odes, war-songs, elegies, and the like, as under: Ad an. 937. THE BATTLE OF BRUNNANBURH, celebrating the great victory of Æthelstan over the combined Norse and Scottish forces, 144 lines; A. 941, an ode in honour of KING EDMUND, 26 lines; A. 958, on EDGAR'S SUCCESSION, 51 lines; A. 973, on EDGAR'S CORONATION at Akemanscester, or Bath, 39 lines; A. 975, on EDGAR'S DEATH, 74 lines; A. 979, on KING EDWARD'S MURDER, 34 lines; A. 1011, on THE SEIZURE OF ARCHB. ELPHEGE, 11 lines; A. 1036, on GODWIN'S MISDEEDS, and CNUT'S DEATH, 40 lines; A. 1057, on THE DEATH OF EDWARD THE ETHELING, 34 lines; A. 1065, on EDWARD'S DEATH and HAROLD'S SUCCESSION, 68 lines, after which the Saxon muse is silent for ever.

The Sax. Chr. was edited first by Abraham Wheloc, Cambridge, 1644, and again by Rev. James Ingram, London, 1823, who collated all known MSS. But the best editions are Earle's two parallel text, 1865, and Benjamin Thorpe's,   870–
London, 1861: language mostly Southern, between . . 1154

THE MENOLOGIUM, a poetical Calendar, Cott. Tib. B. I. ed. Samuel Fox, London, 1830, Ebeling in his Ags. Lesebuch, 1847, and Grein, Vol. II. . . . . 900?

ST. MARIA ÆGYPTIACA: one of the two 'Gloucester fragments,' edited with photozincographic facsimiles by J. Earle, London, 1861—three leaves defective, West Saxon, referred by editor to about 925

St. Swiðhun: the second 'Gloucester fragment,' three leaves, also West Saxon, referred to early part of Æðelred's reign, say 985

The Death of Byrhtnoð, known also as the Battle of Maldon, a spirited historical ode. Cott. Otho A. 12; 690 lines, slightly defective at beginning and end; ed. Grein, Vol. I. in 325 long lines—composed soon after the death of the hero, Byrhtnoð, who fell at the battle of Maldon, Essex, in . . 993

The four Gospels in *West Saxon*, in two MSS.: I. Corp. Cam. by one Ælfric in the Monastery of Bath, about the year 1000; II. Hatton, Oxford, which seems to be a later copy of same, about 1050. . . . . 1000 1050

The four Gospels in *Northumbrian*, partly glosses, partly independent translations (not all glosses, as Skeat wrongly supposes in pref. to his ed. of Mark, 1871). Extant in two MSS.: I. The Lindisfarne, or 'Durham Book,' Cott. Nero D. 4, Latin text by Eadfrith, b. of Lindisfarne about 700, Anglian interlinear translation and gloss by Aldred, 250 years later. II. The Rushworth MSS., of which Matthew and one chapter of Mark are an independent continuous version, *not a gloss*. The rest is a more recent copy of the Lindisfarne MS., Latin text 750, translation and gloss about 975 . 950– 975

Note.—Synoptical editions of these four West Saxon and Northumbrian Gospels begun by Kemble (Matthew, Cambridge, 1858), and continued by Skeat (Mark, London and Cambridge, 1871; Luke, 1874).

Ælfric: either the Archb. of Canterbury (d. 1006) or far more probably the Ælfric, pupil of Ethelwold, b. of Winchester, and elected Abbot of Cerne in Dorsetshire, 1005. To him a large number of works are referred, amongst which two series of Homilies, 40 in each, ed. by Thorpe, 2 vols., 1843-6; a Colloquy, Cott. Tib. A. III., and St. John's, Oxford; a Latin Grammar in Saxon, with a glossary, ed. by W. Somner, Oxford, 1659; all about 1000

The Passion of St. George, in a Cambridge MS. edited with a translation by Rev. C. Hardwick, for the Percy Society, vol. 28, London, 1850—attributed by editor to Ælfric, Archbishop of York, between 1023-1051, say 1025

The Legend of St. Edmund, in prose, ed. Thorpe in his *Analecta Anglo-Saxonica*, and regarded by him as East-Anglian, about 1080

SOLOMON AND SATURN, 506 lines, in two defective MSS., Corp. 422, and Corp. 41, on margin of Alfred's Beda, written about end of eleventh century, ed. Grein, vol. II. . . . 1090?

NOTE ON THE VERCELLI AND EXETER CODICES.

These are the great store-houses of Saxon poetry, containing everything of consequence still extant, except the BEOWULF, the JUDITH, the METRICAL PSALTER, and the PARAPHRASES attributed to Cadmon. THE VERCELLI MS. was first brought to light in a convent of that town by Dr. Frederick Blume in 1823, whose timely discovery of its great value saved it from a slow process of destruction. In his Iter Italicum, I. 99, apud Grein, I. 364, he tells us that the monks, supposing it a work of St. Eusebius, bishop of Vercelli in the fourth century, were in the habit of tearing out portions of it as relics for distribution amongst his votaries: hence its present mangled state. Besides the poems above mentioned under Cynewulf, it contains: THE FATE OF THE APOSTLES, 95 lines; TWO ADDRESSES OF THE SOUL TO THE BODY, 128 and 168 lines (the first found also in the Exeter MS.), and a fragment on THE FALSEHOOD OF THE WORLD (*Bî Manna Léâse*).

THE EXETER MS. (so called because placed by Leofric, first bishop of Exeter, in the Cathedral Library in 1046, when the see was transferred thither from Crediton) is also defective, the first seven leaves and the end, besides several pages in the body, being lost or cut out. It has been fully described by Wanley (in Hickes's Thesaurus), and by Conybeare (1826), and edited with a full English translation, as the CODEX EXONIENSIS, by B. Thorpe for the Society of Antiquaries, London, 1842—also mostly by Grein, I. and II. Besides the works above quoted it contains a number of smaller pieces, such as: THE RHYMING POEM, 87 lines; CHRIST AND SATAN, 733 lines; THE WONDERS OF CREATION, 102 lines; THE PANTHER, 74 lines; THE WHALE, 89 lines; THE PARTRIDGE, 16 lines; THE HUSBAND'S MESSAGE, 52 lines; DOMES DÆG, 119 lines; CHRIST'S DESCENT, 137 lines; MANNA CRAEFTAS, 113 lines; MANNA MÓD, 84 lines; MANNA WYRDE, 98 lines; THE AZARIAS, 191 lines; ALMS, 8 lines; PHARAOH, 9 lines; GNOMIC VERSES. Grein refers this codex to 'the first half of eleventh century' (I. p. 365). In the list of Leofric's gifts to his Cathedral, several MSS. of which are extant, this Codex is described as 'I. mẏcel englisc boc be gehwilcum þingum on leoð-wisan geworht,' *i.e.*, one great English book on divers things, wrought in verse.

BROKEN SAXON OR TRANSITION PERIOD: 1066-1200.

THE FORGED CHARTERS in the Bodl. Laud, or Peterborough MS. of the Sax. Chr. inserted at A. 656 and 675, but really written early in the twelfth century, and representing the East-Anglian dialect of that period, say about . . . 1120

THE MORAL ODE, a rhyming homily of about 400 lines, extant in various MSS., of which the Digby printed by Hickes in his 'Thesaurus,' I. p. 222; the Egerton, 613, by Furnivall, in his 'Early E. Poems,' edited for the Philological Society, 1858; the Lambeth, 487 (imperfect), by Dr. Morris, at pp. 158-183 of his Old English Homilies, first series, 1868; the Trinity Cam. B. 14-52, by same in second series, 1873, pp. 220-232. In pref. to first series Morris says, 'I am inclined to think that all existing copies of this ode are taken from an older (Saxon-English) version, which may perhaps turn up hereafter.' The oldest extant may date from 1150

CNUT'S SONG, preserved by Thomas, monk of Ely, in his History of the Church of Ely, written after 1166, say about . 1170

EARLY ENGLISH HOMILIES, in the first series, from Lambeth and other MSS., ed. Morris for Early English Text Society, 1867, mostly in Southern dialects of twelfth century, say between 1130–75

EARLY ENGLISH HOMILIES, second series, from the Trin. MS. B. 14-52, with later hymns (thirteenth century), from Corp. MS. 54 D. 4-14, ed. Morris for E. E. T. S., 1868, mostly Essex dialect, say about 1180

THE HATTON GOSPELS, based on the West Saxon versions mentioned above at A. 1000-1050. Matthew published by Hardwick, 1858 . . . . 1180?

LAYAMON'S enlarged version of Wace's Brut, 32,000 short lines, alliterative with occasional rhymes, extant in two MSS.: I. Cott. Caligula A. IX. representing the Worcestershire or West of England dialect, about the year 1200
II. Cott. Otho, C. XIII., about fifty years later, say . 1250
Editio Princeps, Sir F. Madden's, 3 vols., London, 1847.

THE ORMULUM, by Orrmin, a metrical paraphrase of the Gospels, with comments, 20,000 lines, in one MS. Bodleian, referred to the reign of John—published by Robt. Meadows White, 2 vols., Oxford, 1852, represents the East Anglian speech at beginning of thirteenth century, say . . . 1210

EARLY ENGLISH PERIOD: 1200–1300.

SEINTE MARHARETE, the Legend of St. Margaret, MS. in Trin. Coll. Cam., edited for E. E. T. S. by Rev. O. Cockayne, 1866. Oxfordshire or South Midland dialect of thirteenth century . . . . 1220?

HALI MEIDENHAD, ed. Cockayne for E. E. T. S., 1866. West Midland of same period . . . . . 1230?

ON GOD OREISUN, Cott. Nero, A. XIV.
ON LOFSONG OF URE LEFDI, *ib.*
ON LOFSONG OF URE LOUERDE, *ib.*
SAWLES WARDE, Bodl. 34, Royal MS. 17, A. 27.
ÞE WOHUNGE OF URE LAUERD, Cott. Tit. D. 18, West Midland.

All edited by Dr. Morris for E. E. T. S. in Early English Homilies, first series, parts I. and II., 1868, representing generally the language of the thirteenth century, say about . . 1250

RELIGIOUS POEMS, &c., in the *Liber de Antiquis Legibus*, belonging to the Corporation of London, and representing the London speech of thirteenth century: say 1250

THE ANCREN RIWLE, a prose treatise on the duties of Convent life in four MSS.: one in Corp. Cam. and three in Brit. Mus.: Nero A. XIV., Titus D. XVIII., and Cleopatra C. VI. The first of these ed. by Rev. James Morton for the Camden Society, London, 1853. The MSS. differ considerably in spelling and other respects, but represent the Dorset and other Southern varieties generally of thirteenth century, say . . 1220–50

THE BESTIARY, 800 lines, translated by a bishop Theobald from a Latin 'Physiologus,' in an OLD ENGLISH MISCELLANY, ed. Dr. Morris for E. E. T. S., 1872. East Midland, about . 1250

NOTE.—This Miscellany contains also a number of KENTISH Sermons, PROVERBS (popularly attributed to Alfred), and some RELIGIOUS POEMS, from the Jesus MS., mainly representing the language of thirteenth century.

Appendix II.

GENESIS AND EXODUS, a rhyming poem of 4,160 octosyllabic lines, in a Corpus MS., ed. Morris for E. E. T. S. 1865. Suffolk or East Midland . . . . 1250?

THE ATHANASIAN CREED, in a North Lincolnshire dialect, printed by Hickes, Thesaurus, I. 233, about 1250

THE LORD'S PRAYER, HAIL MARY, and CREED, from an East Midland MS., printed in the *Reliquiæ Antiquæ*, I. 22 . 1250

THE OWL AND NIGHTINGALE, a rhyming poem of 1,700 octosyllabic lines, by Nicholas of Guildford, in two MSS. : first in Jesus, Oxford ; second, Cott. Caligula, A. IX. 5, fol. 230 (same MS. as that containing Layamon's early text), both in a West of England dialect, ed. Stratmann, 1871, Percy Society, No. 39, not later than 1250

THE CUCKOO'S SONG, 12 lines, in Harl. MSS. 978, f. 5— the oldest English song with MS. musical notes, ed. Ellis for Phil. Society, 1868 . . . . 1250?

ST. SWIÐHUN (a metrical life of), in the Bodl. Laud MS. 463, fol. 63, and edited with the above-mentioned 'Gloucester Fragments,' by J. Earle, London, 1861—138 lines, referred to thirteenth century, say about 1250

THE HUNTINGDON PROCLAMATION—the first document in English on the Patent Rolls, which date from the third of John, 1202. It is a parliamentary writ issued in forty-second of Hen. III. to every shire in England, that of Huntingdon being still extant. Carefully printed in North Br. Rev. for June, 1868, also by A. J. Ellis, for Philological Society, 1873. Important as the first specimen of Early English bearing a certain date, viz., Oct. 18th 1258

HAVELOK THE DANE, a metrical version of Gaimar's 'Lai de Aveloc,' in a Bodl. MS. first published with the French text and a glossary by Sir Fr. Madden, London, 1828, and re-edited for E. E. T. S. by Rev. W. W. Skeat, 1868, represents the East Midland dialect of latter portion of thirteenth century, say about 1270

SIR TRISTRAM, a metrical version of a small part of the French Romance, wrongly ascribed by Sir Walter Scott to the Northern poet Thomas of Ercildoun. It is *Southern* . . 1280?

THE NORTHUMBRIAN PSALTER, metrical, published by the Surtees Society. The language is Northern, and referable to this period, though the MS. is fifty or sixty years later . 1280?

KING HORN, an Early English Romance of 1,600 lines, first published d'après les MSS. [Harl. 2,253, &c.] de Londres, de Cambridge, d'Oxford, et d'Edimbourg, par F. Michel, Paris, 1854 ; also by Rev. J. R. Lumby for E. E. T. S. 1866—second half of thirteenth century, say 1275

FLORIS AND BLANCHEFLOUR, and THE ASSUMPCIOUN, in the King Horn MS. ed. by Lumby for E. E. T. S., 1866 . 1275

GUY OF WARWICK and COLBROND THE DANE, an Anglo-Danish subject, attributed to Walter of Exeter, ed. from the Auchinleck MS. in the Advocates' Library, Edinburgh, by Turnbull, 1840 . . . . 1280?

THE HARROWING OF HELL, the earliest extant specimen of an English drama (Chester series), edited by Dr. Mall, of Breslau, who collated three MSS.: a Warwickshire, 1290 ; a Herefordshire, 1313 ; and a Northern, 1330. There is also a Harleian, 2,013. East Midland 1280

KYNG ALIXAUNDER—a version of a French poem now lost, in irregular rhymes of six, eight, and even more syllables— ed. Weber, Metrical Romances I. Midland, about . . 1280

EARLY ENGLISH POEMS, including several HAGIOLOGIES, edited by Furnivall for Phil. Soc. Contains *St. Dunstan, An Oxford Student, The Jews and the Cross, St. Swithin, St. Kenelm, St. James, St. Christopher, The* 11,000 *Virgins, St. Edmund the Confessor, St. Edmund the King, St. Katharine, St. Andrew, St. Lucie, St. Edward, Judas Iscariot, Pilate* . 1290

THE HOLY RODE, in ' Legends of the Holy Rood, Symbols of the Passion and Cross, &c.,' ed. Morris for E. E. T. S., 1871—before 1300, say 1290

ROBERT OF GLOUCESTER'S CHRONICLE, in Alexandrines, from siege of Troy to death of Hen. III., 1272—the first history of England in English—ed. Thos. Hearne from a Harl. MS., with a continuation from a Cott. MS., in 2 vols., Oxford, 1724, represents the West Midland speech of the end of thirteenth century. Concluded about 12

By him also : ' Lives and Legends of English Saints,' including the murder of Thomas à Becket and the voyage of St. Brandan, published by the Percy Soc., vols. XIV. and XIX.

THE PROVERBS OF HENDYNG, a series of moral sayings in six-syllabled rhyming stanzas, each concluding with the refrain '*quoth Hendyng*,' Harl. MS. 2,253, published in Kemble's

Appendix II.

Anglo-Saxon Dialogues (Ælfric Soc., No. 14, p. 270). Southern . . . . 1300?

THE LAND OF COCKAYNE, a satirical poem, attacking monkish luxury (whence the title, *coquina* = a kitchen), Egerton and More MSS., Cambridge, 784, f. 1, published in Hickes's Thesaurus, and by Furnivall in E. E. Poems and Lives of the Saints . . . . 1300?

ROBERT MANNYNG, of Brunne, in Lincolnshire: I. THE HANDLYNG SYNNE, a free and enlarged version of William of Waddington's 'Manuel des Péchés,' is *the first readable English*, its language being greatly in advance of his contemporaries and even of his immediate followers, thus forming a great landmark in the history of the English tongue—edited for the Roxburghe Club from the Bodl. and Brit. Mus. MSS. by F. J. Furnivall, London, 1862. East Midland, date fixed by himself at 1303

II. THE CHRONICLE, a metrical version of Peter Langtoft's French rhyming Chronicle, ed. Thos. Hearne, Oxford, 1725. Composed between 1327 1338

III. THE MEDITACIOUNS ON THE LORD'S SUPPER, probably by him, ed. J. M. Cowper for E. E. T. S., 1875.

Mannyng closes the strictly Early English Period, or rather opens a new era, connecting the foregoing with the Middle English and Chaucerian epoch. With him also closes the further growth of the Teutonic element in English.* But on the other hand with him, and about his time, begins the steady inflow of foreign elements, Norman first, and then Latin, ending mainly with Gibbon.

---

* '*Since, nor, its, unless, below, until,* are our main Teutonic changes since Manning's time.'—*Oliphant, Standard English*, p. 186.

www.ingramcontent.com/pod-product-compliance
Lightning Source LLC
Chambersburg PA
CBHW021727220426
43662CB00008B/737